PREDATORY
FEMALE

ii

"REVEREND SHANNON'S CLASSIC, *THE PREDATORY FEMALE,* STANDS FOR ALL TIME AS THE DEFINITIVE WORK IN ITS FIELD. A MASTERPIECE!"

—*Rohok Q. Bap*

"ONE OF ITS KIND. A MONUMENT TO LIBERTY! POWERFUL AND HUMOROUS.

—*Rolando Filigree*

"SCANDALOUS! LIKE EATING CANDY! BRILLIANT. A REFRESHING DELIGHT.

—*Dr. Hammond Diewelder*

"OUTRAGEOUS! AN UTTERLY COMPELLING WORK. CANDID AND SPELLBINDING, THERE'S NOTHING LIKE IT ANYWHERE!"

—*Obal F. Loon*

"WONDERFUL! IT'S ABOUT TIME! MARVELOUSLY WRITTEN AND ENGROSSING, I COULDN'T PUT IT DOWN.

—*Fortunado "Jazzbro" Lucrecci*

THE
PREDATORY
FEMALE

A FIELD GUIDE TO DATING AND THE MARRIAGE-DIVORCE INDUSTRY

REV. LAWRENCE SHANNON

iv

Published by Banner Books, Inc.
BANNER BOOKS, INC.
P.O. Box 70302
Reno, Nevada 89570

Manufactured in the United States of America

ISBN 0-9615938-0-6

Fourth Printing

Dedicated to those who have lined their
pockets with spoils from the largest
camouflaged scam in the history of the
free world: *Marriage.*

"The heart is deceitful above all things, and
desperately wicked: who can know it?"

–Jer. 17:9

THIS BOOK IS **NOT**
RECOMMENDED BY THE FOLLOWING . . .

- National Organization of Women
- American Bar Association
- Rev. Jerry Falwell
- Marvin Mitchelson
- The League of Women Voters
- National Association of Trial Lawyers
- Daughters of the American Revolution
- American Medical Association
- College of Obstetricians and Gynecologists
- National Council of Churches
- Dr. Joyce Bozo

It is an accurate observation of a world groaning from a heavenly curse to say a happy and truly fit relationship between a man and woman is miraculous. The path to such a blessed union is fraught with almost insurmountable barriers. Certainly the very fact of our high birth rate is a product of the disregard of all proper conditions for mating, being rather a case of any port in a storm.

—Rev. Shannon speaking to friends
Los Angeles, California 1981

Gentlemen, when in the field, have *The Predatory Female* available for quick reference. Before encountering a predatory female you may wish to review the applicable pages. This will sharpen your skills at identifying her and countering her moves. She is a master of her craft and you'll need all the help you can get. Take heed, for her passion is ten times fiercer than yours and full of madness.

—from a speech by Rev. Shannon
Ft. Worth, Texas   1982

Victims of the predatory female are strewn all over the nation, writing alimony checks, recovering from gunshot wounds, treating cat scratches, trying to see their children, paying attorney's fees, picking through the detritus of their lives, and struggling to recover from ruined years. Hopefully, by hearing the screams from inside the well, we can avoid falling in ourselves.

—from a radio interview with Rev. Shannon

NOTICE

The opinions expressed in this book are the product of thousands of real life experiences and are not an attempt to proffer legal advice.

Table of Contents

Introduction

pred·a·to·ry (prĕd′ə-tôre′, -tōr′ē) *adj.* [Lat. *praedatoris*< *praedari* to plunder<*praeda,* booty.] **1.** Of, pertaining to, or characterized by plundering, pillaging, or marauding. **2.** Preying on other animals: PREDACIOUS. **3.** Marked by a tendency to victimize or destroy others for one's own benefit.—**pred′a·to′ri·ly** *adv.*—**pred′a·to′ri·ness** *n.*

She was a spring bride, a graceful beauty radiating health and happiness. The garden wedding overlooked the blue Pacific on a lovely day. The groom, young and handsome, smiled lovingly as they repeated their vows. Truly they were a storybook couple with a charming future.

Fifteen months later, the bride's attorney was demanding alimony, community property, attorney's fees, court costs, child custody, child support, and more. The groom's attorney responded, setting off a bitter divorce lasting longer than the marriage.

What happened? Could their relationship, like thousands every year, have been founded upon a misunderstanding? More people are answering yes to that question as it becomes increasingly evident that we are wading in the pathos of marital disaster in this country. Let's face it, you can't even buy a bag of groceries today without getting a short course in divorce from the tabloids at the checkout counter.

But what primary misconception can be blamed for the growing war zone between the sexes?

It is the quiet, festering, and popular ignorance of the predatory female. Her perfidious nature has persistently escaped proper scrutiny and exposure throughout most of this century. The predatory female, obfuscated by society and custom, is misunderstood by females and males alike. It is this lack of awareness that eventually leads most couples to the brink of catastrophe.

Look at a typical day's headlines: MAN SHOOTS WIFE, THEN SELF. LOVER'S QUARREL ENDS IN DEATH. GIRLFRIEND SUES FOR ALIMONY. INFANT ABANDONED AT DRIVE-IN. SHOOTING ENDS LOVE TRIANGLE. DIVORCE ERUPTS IN VIOLENCE. DISTRAUGHT FATHER STEALS OWN CHILD.

A working knowledge of the predatory female can greatly aid everyone in avoiding these terrible, but common events.

We live in a matriarchal society. Most of our citizens are females. Can we afford to remain blinded to an inherent trait of most of our citizens? A study of the predatory female is long overdue. We must learn to recognize and deal with her. These pages can help their readers avoid the misery and self-destruction inflicted daily upon the victims of the predatory female.

There is no other book like this in the world. Similar works have been censored and destroyed. The unspoken and chilling menace that emanates from the predatory females of our society has, until now, kept the facts herein concealed.

In the following chapters, the true predatory female is publicly unveiled for the first time. You will learn to recognize and avoid her traps. You will explore all phases of dealing with predatory females, from casual acquaintances to post-divorce relations.

After reviewing the characteristics of predatory females in Section I, you will be ready for the Survival Guides in Section II. These will help protect you from the ever present dangers in a society that is crawling with predatory females. Hopefully, if you comprehend and retain the contents of these sections, you'll be saved from the matriarchal sludge pile, from eventually becoming an embittered, cynical old grab bag who's had the short course—a human piñata wearing fifty pounds of body jewelry, a velure jump suit, and driving around Marina Del Rey with personalized plates that say "STUD ONE." You may even be rescued from that pathetic mob of hungry, searching males who, strutting and preening, descend nightly upon the profusion of singles bars, swinging their scrotums like Argentine bolas.

But be warned. Those with fairy tale ideas of courtship and marriage may find these pages upsetting. Being no less candid than a process server, the author relies on naked frankness. Consequently, this material doesn't cater to the fainthearted. It's for people desiring the truth about their circumstances, who prefer reality to fiction, and who base their decisions on facts rather than dreams.

There are many publications designed to help people attract the opposite sex, set up housekeeping with their lovers, prepare for marriage, or rebuild their lives after divorce. These books deal with the results of mistakes. *The Predatory Female* teaches how to avoid such mistakes in the first place.

Some people aren't comfortable with reality and may initially reject the message herein, preferring to perpetuate the myths and fantasies concealing predatory females. The smoke screen, in place for thousands of years, is not forecast to end here, so the only hope for these untutored lambs may be that Reverend Shannon's words get to them before a predatory female does.

Fortunately for those who would guard their lives, property, and sanity against dangerous temporary euphorias, there is the still small voice of reason. You are about to hear that voice. Read, enjoy, laugh, but most of all . . . remember.

> "I beheld the wretch—the
> miserable monster whom I had created."

> —*Mary Shelley*

> "Every dog has his day, but
> the night belongs to us."
> —*a Predatory Female*

SECTION I

TRAITS OF THE PREDATORY FEMALE

INITIAL CONSIDERATIONS

"Everything that deceives
may be said to enchant."

—*Plato*

Earmarks

Q. Can the predatory female be identified in our society?

A. Fortunately, yes. Although it's impossible to categorize all behavior in a segment of population, there are discernible traits in the predatory female that, once learned, may serve as warning signals to the enlightened.

Q. Who benefits by learning these traits?

A. Everyone, but males have the edge in the present legal climate.

Q. Why?

A. Men, poorly educated about predatory females, are notoriously clumsy when dealing with them. Our earliest history bristles with examples of strong, intelligent men outwitted and destroyed by females in the predatory mode. This continues presently where women, victims of their own predatory natures and aided by the court system, are responsible for the ruin of families, businesses, and lives all over the nation.

Q. Are you blaming women exclusively for these disasters?

A. No. Little of the mayhem could occur without the endless army of men, untutored in the predatory female, queuing up obediently for destruction. Blinded by steam from their own gonads, they stumble ignorantly into relationships with women and later awaken to find themselves trapped in an ever deepening pit of emotional, legal, and financial quicksand.

Me, Myself, and I

Q. How do we begin to identify a predatory female?

A. One giveaway is that she flatly represents the self-centered faction of the population. While a male gravitates towards things and activities, a predatory female is primarily concerned with herself. Since the publishing industry is extremely sensitive to readers' interests, a glance at any news stand will help explain. Publications designed for men bear titles like *Sports, Flying, Electronics, Mechanics*, etc., while those sold mainly to females are called *Self, Glamour, Image, Me, Woman,* and so forth. The predatory female is concerned chiefly with herself and what others think of her. This is a basic rule. A picture of a cat, spending hours licking itself, comes to mind.

Unhampered By Ego

Q. Are you saying the predatory female is an egomaniac?

A. Not at all. The predatory female rarely exhibits an ego the way males do. Her ego has given way to convenience and practicality. Moreover, she is quietly amazed at the excessiveness of the male ego. Unhampered by ego, she is quicker and more adroit than the male. It is curious how the female will sometimes berate the male about his ego when that very weakness often enables her to control him. Again, the predatory female is not ultimately concerned with what men think of her, only what women think. Keep in mind the old sayings that "a woman needs a man like a fish needs a bicycle," and "women undress for men but dress for women."

Helter Skelter

Q. Beyond herself and her status with other women, does anything else pique her interest?

A. Yes, any combination of money, romance, and excitement. The scent of these accommodations will have her rising like a cobra from a wicker basket. The provider of such diversions occupies center stage in her life, but his identity is unimportant to her, and it's a temporary position. Nobody can amuse her forever. All pied pipers eventually fade into the past.

What About Love?

Q. You haven't mentioned love as an interest of the predatory female. Why?
A. The predatory female never loves a man; she only loves the love. This is a basic rule.

The Adversary

Q. Who is the adversary?
A. This is a role automatically adopted by the predatory female whenever she is with a man. She loves to constantly prod him and fence with him. If he fails to respond acceptably, she deems him unromantic and dull. His services will soon be terminated. The adversary phenomenon is closely related to the "defense of the nest" discussed later.

Will The Real Predatory Female Please Stand Up?

Q. How else might one recognize a predatory female?
A. The predatory nature resides in almost every woman, but is not always visible. It isn't

constantly at the surface of their personalities, producing elongated eye teeth. You may deal with a woman for some time without seeing any predatory signs. But if you're patient, and take time to study the female in question, you'll eventually see the predatory nature emerge. At times, even for the seasoned observer, this can be an unnerving experience.

Q. Reverend Shannon, do you use the words "female," "predatory female," and "woman" interchangeably?

A. In this book, yes.

Q. Why?

A. Because it most closely approximates the real world.

The Acquisitive Mode

Q. What is the acquisitive mode?

A. It is the yawn of the predatory nature, a primal stirring. It may rise slowly to the surface—a monster from the lagoon, or it might blind side you like a bear charging out of the broom closet. The mode can be triggered by many things. She suddenly wants to get married. She is bored. Her best friend got married, she doesn't like her job, she wants to move into better housing, she just turned thirty, her sister got engaged, or a host of other reasons. Her invisible electronic gun sight begins sweeping the range, scanning to acquire a target.

Q. How can you be sure a woman is in the acquisitive mode?
A. She shows interest in men. This is a positive identification.

The Primal Woman

Q. Are the young women of America a collection of scheming mercenaries?
A. Hardly. The majority are only doing what comes naturally and what they've been taught by their mothers. That is to manipulate the multitudes of hapless men who continue to rush eagerly into servitude as they have for thousands of years. Usually her scheming is minimal, and indeed, when she behaves naturally, when she relies wholly upon her primordial instincts, she is most effective. The primal woman is so beguiling and disarming that she is infinitely dangerous.

The Supernatural

Q. Why do you equate associating with a predatory female to dabbling in the black arts?
A. It is one of mankind's strongest historical parallels. In the Garden of Eden, it was Eve who had the rapport with the Serpent. The Witch at Endor was a woman. Ancient literature, like Homer, expresses the supernatural leanings of females. Nothing has changed.

For example, a modern predatory female has the uncanny ability to track you, in person or by phone, to the remotest parts of the earth. When you begin to fraternize with a woman, you are taking the first steps in a ritual mating dance that, if allowed to progress, will result in your moving about the floor in a semi-comatose state until you are fleeced of your money, property, and peace of mind. A predatory female will study you. She learns to know what you are thinking. She begins the strongest primeval death grip known to mankind.

Q. Can reading this book cause problems with a current lover?

A. Reading and comprehending *The Predatory Female* results in "knowing too much" by the standards of a predatory female. Unless you are able to conceal your knowledge, she will discover you and recoil like a vampire from a crucifix.

The Real Lesson In The Garden

Q. What is the real lesson in the garden?

A. Adam and Eve were instructed not to eat the fruit of the tree. The Devil evidently studied both humans to find which would be easiest to tempt, the least stable. Consequently, Eve was tricked into eating the fruit. But remember, Eve was tricked; Adam was not. The real lesson is that Adam, seeing the banishment of Eve, purposely gobbled the fruit because he couldn't stand to be without her. Rather than be left alone, he skulked to the tree, and, with both eyes wide open, munched his way to damnation. History's first grovel. Adam groveled to avert loneliness. Even today, thousands of men are flushing their lives and fortunes, usually into the marriage mill, to avoid being left by, or without, a woman.

The Chameleon Syndrome

Q. What is the chameleon syndrome?
A. A quasi-supernatural transformation, the chameleon syndrome is the predatory female's unholy ability to become whatever the script calls for in "hooking" a man. She will adopt his viewpoints, his attitudes, his hobbies, and his dislikes. Her personality will change to suit his. She will enroll in classes, become a gourmet cook, stop smoking, switch religions, accept his friends, humor his jealousies, develop a relationship with his relatives, or whatever else is called for. She will change colors in the rocks like a chameleon! Of all the traits exhibited by predatory females, this chameleon syndrome is one of the most lethal.
Q. Why?
A. Because, amazingly, the predatory female is completely sincere about her new behavior. She isn't consciously aware of any deception.

She transforms involuntarily. She could take a lie detector test and pass. There is nothing crooked in her mind. Consequently the male detects nothing amiss because there is nothing amiss. Everything is normal and natural. The predatory female has matched herself with the surrounding landscape; she adapted to her environment for mating and survival. The male innocently concludes he has met the "right" woman.

At The Stroke Of Midnight

Q. How long does the chameleon syndrome last?

A. As long as it takes to subdue the male, which usually means the bonds of holy matrimony and the enforcement powers of the judicial system.

Q. Then what happens?

A. The adaptation is no longer necessary, the spell is broken, and the colors begin changing back to original. "We've grown apart," is the familiar statement. "Our values have changed." In truth, the chameleon has simply relaxed to its natural, more comfortable exterior.

Q. You say "more comfortable exterior." Are you implying the predatory female is uncomfortable in the adapted colors?

A. Although unaware of it, she is often ill at ease. Most people have seen an acquisitive

woman working hard to bring a man to the
altar. She may lose weight, become nervous
and fidgety, cry a lot, or develop insomnia.
These are signs of a chameleon chafing in her
temporary exterior and compose more trade-
marks of a predatory female.

Disguises

Q. Do predatory females physically disguise
themselves?
A. Yes. The predatory female habitually em-
ploys subterfuge. Each morning across America, millions of females don disguises. They
use make-up, wigs, face paint, phony eye-
brows, false eye lashes, eye shadow, lipstick,
false fingernails, hair color, corsets, sprays,
and other camouflage. Women's clothing de-
signers often refer to the "illusion" they are
creating. Occasionally these females improve
their appearance, but the fact remains they
are hiding something. They are fooling somebody. The practice is so commonplace that
few see it for what it is: deception.

> "All women, whatever age, rank, profession
> or degree, whether virgins, maids or widows,
> that shall impose upon, seduce or betray into
> matrimony any of His Majesty's subjects, by
> scents, paints, cosmetics, washes, artificial
> teeth, false hair, iron stave hoops, high-
> heeled shoes, bolstered hips, or padded

bosoms shall incur the penalty of the law enforced against witchcraft and like misdemeanors and, upon conviction, that marriage shall stand null and void."

—Act of British Parliament—1770

Q. Besides outright deception, are there other negative aspects to these disguises?

A. Not only are regiments of men conditioned to subsidize these female diversionary tactics, but heavy users of the cosmetic disguises are simply unclean. They leave streaks of make-up and lipstick on clothes and bed sheets, they often improperly mix the various substances (creating a noxious odor), and some individuals host a form of microscopic mite in their eyelids. Amusingly, for all their trouble, a large percentage of these females succeed only in adding a Halloween aspect to their appearance.

Q. Are there other forms of disguises?

A. Yes, in the sense that a predatory female is adept at disguising her *intentions.* This is more fully discussed later, but here's an example that gives a good insight into the female thinking process: Recently a TV crew interviewed customers of a new co-ed health spa in Dallas. The place was packed with nubile, available ladies and gentlemen, all dancing, stretching, pumping iron, and swimming to the beat of rock music. In response to questions, several young ladies said, "There's a lot of cute guys here, and when we go out with them WE DON'T FEEL LIKE WE'VE BEEN PICKED UP. It's not like a singles bar. It's a more comfortable, easy way to meet people.'' In other words, the ladies were more comfortable when their amicabilities weren't as obvious, when their intentions toward the opposite sex were couched in a deceiving framework or DISGUISED.

The Pack

Q. Do predatory females run in packs?
A. Yes, most predatory creatures do. Sharks and hyenas are good examples. Predatory females are comfortable in packs. Have you ever seen a woman excuse herself from a group, to go to the bathroom, only to be followed by the other women? This is packing. They like to gossip and scheme out of earshot. Predatory females rely heavily on the consensus of the pack and thereby encounter difficulty in making individual decisions. The pack includes their mothers and girlfriends and constitutes the sole governing body in the life of a predatory female. The blessing or cursing of the pack (a committee decision), is largely determinate in the rise and fall of lovers, husbands, and gynecologists.

> "Man comes from the womb and spends the rest of his life trying to get back there."
>
> —*George Bernard Shaw*

The Matriarchal System

Q. What is the matriarchal system?

A. Like open range to a wolf, it is the operating medium of the predatory female. It is the unspoken mass thought process that supports her activities. Through the incontestable voting power of superior numbers of women, it controls politics, the media, and the church. Firmly entrenched, the matriarchal system is apple pie, motherhood, and the marriage-divorce industry. Nearly every citizen, like it or not, nourishes it. With a supporting cast of thousands including lawyers, doctors, clergy, and politicians, its influence reaches all phases of American life as it forever perpetuates the power of the predatory female. But even with the overwhelming voting power of females and their subsequent control of governmental functions, the matriarchal system could never operate efficiently without the hordes of male drones it has created. These men, preconditioned by their mothers and suffering from a self-imposed order of chivalry, consistently front for the system and its predatory female masters.

Q. An example?

A. The male dominated Supreme Court recently refused to allow the conscription of women into the armed services. The courts, fronted by male drones, are overjoyed at the prospect of helping a predatory female collect her alimony. But when it comes to the dirty work of protecting the very system fostering this alimony, they turn to the vast reserve of perpetual victims: the befuddled males.

Q. How could this system ever get started?

A. Prior to the turn of the century, the foundation was already in place with the popular pastime of glorifying and deifying the female. But shortly after 1900, when women were emancipated by a quaking and groveling male population, the female block took a subtle and permanent stranglchold on the legal process. Historically, a strong matriarchal system is always present in a morally declining society. Moreover, the higher standard of living a nation enjoys, the more likely it is to have an entrenched matriarchal system.

Q. If that's true, why did the Equal Rights Amendment fail?

A. We may have a case of overkill here, so the female masters of the system have disagreed on the issue. Two thirds of the state legislatures haven't ratified it, creating a wave of additional propaganda, but enough laws are already on the books to insure equal rights.

Bag Check

Q. Is shoplifting a habit of the predatory female?

A. The stealing of items from stores, restaurants, hotels, and places of employment is considered acceptable behavior by predatory females. This habit also extends to your home. Indeed, the unmasked predatory female is practically amoral and she doesn't improve with age.

> "Therefore a woman who is perfectly truthful and not given to dissimulation is perhaps an impossibility, and for this very reason they are so quick at seeing through dissimulation in others that it is not a wise thing to attempt it with them. But this fundamental defect which I have stated, with all that it entails, gives rise to falsity, faithlessness, treachery, ingratitude, and so on. Perjury in a court of justice is more often committed by women than by men. It may, indeed, be generally questioned whether women ought to be sworn at all. From time to time one finds repeated cases everywhere of ladies, who want for nothing, taking things from shop-counters when no one is looking, and making off with them."

—Arthur Schopenhauer   *1788-1860*

Soaps

Q. How are predatory females and soap operas associated?

A. TV soap operas are particularly attractive to predatory females. Their lifestyles reflect an almost unconscious imitation of soap opera scenarios. A predatory female enjoys cultivating scandalous events and involving herself in everyone's problems. A group of predatory females will even talk like soap opera players, whispering in conspiratorial tones and using exaggerated voice inflections. The alert observer can identify this predatory sign in almost any gathering of females.

Ding

Q. What is a ding?
A. Listening for dings is a good way to spot predatory females because they are a universal trait of the creature. Unfortunately, a man usually listens to very little of what a woman says. With other matters on his mind, like sex, he doesn't carefully consider her words. This is a mistake. On a date, though he is primarily occupied by pulling money from his wallet, he should train himself to listen carefully. Eventually she will say something that doesn't make any sense. This is a ding. He may have to listen for several hours, but it's worth it. Sooner or later, if she is a predatory female, she'll make a statement that doesn't jibe. If you happen to be the listener, mentally register a DING. As your skill improves, and with more exposure, you may be hearing dings constantly. After you've heard a few, they become easier to identify. A ding alerts you to being in the presence of a predatory female.

The Volcano

Q. Are irrational acts a trait of the predatory female?

A. Yes. She is capable of sudden, illogical, and self-destructive acts at any moment. She is totally unpredictable.

Q. Why is this?

A. Examine a cervix. It is symbolic. With the appearance of a miniature, upside down volcano, it is the capstone of an area spawning violent chemical and hormonal eruptions. It seems incredulous that anyone subjected to these biological explosions could escape an unstable personality. It is no wonder that predatory females are often at a loss to explain their actions.

Q. Do these facts make it difficult for a predatory female to function in society?

A. Not at all. First, we live in a matriarchal society, totally hospitable to these vagaries, and second, she is attractive, beguiling, and adaptable. Also, legions of males—drones of the matriarchy—festoon the countryside, catering to her every whim.

The Media

Q. How does the media fit into a study of the predatory female?

A. The mass media is an important propaganda arm of the matriarchal society and vital to the predatory female. Twenty four hours a day we are bombarded with songs, commercials, and motion pictures depicting marriage as the ultimate in happiness and achievement. You will never be truly happy unless you are with the "right" woman. Of course you must marry her, too. Later on, if things don't work out, you obviously didn't have the "right" one. She is still out there . . . waiting for you. You must try to find her. Your happiness depends on meeting her. Don't you crave the euphoric, nuptial bliss that your friends and neighbors have found? A million times per second this message is beamed from broadcasting stations all over the country. There is no escaping its harangue. It is small wonder that millions of males, beaten senseless by this propaganda from the matriarchy, have fallen for the scam.

Feline Power

Q. What do predatory females and cats have in common?
A. The similarity between cats and predatory females can hardly be overemphasized. Both are creatures of the night, linked with the black arts, late sleepers, faithful to no one, ungrateful, self-centered, possessed of an uncanny sixth sense, and look strangely different when their hair gets wet. A predatory

female will sometimes blatantly tell you she is a witch or psychic. Coincidentally, it's not unusual for a predatory female's menstrual cycle to align itself with her cat's, or those of her roommates. Remember that although the male is like a dog and loves its predatory female master, even after being kicked, the female is like a cat and never gets emotionally attached to anyone.

The Flash

Q. What is the flash?
A. The flash is a momentary facial expression of the predatory female. It is a surfacing of the predatory fury that is immediately subdued when the creature is acquisitive. Alert observers of the predatory female will occasionally witness one. The flash occurs with little warning and it's a sobering sneak preview, a glimpse into the abyss.
Q. What facial expression portrays the predatory fury?
A. An alien, cold, and completely ruthless one—a look of unemotional murder.
Q. And it quickly subsides?
A. Quickly enough for the unenlightened to dismiss it as preposterous, or miss it altogether.
Q. Can the flash take another form?
A. Yes. Sometimes it's a facial snapshot

looking ten or more years in the future, the viewing of which is shocking.

The Blimp Syndrome

Q. What is the blimp syndrome?
A. Another trait of the predatory female, it describes her startling ability to gain or lose weight rapidly. She may become unrecognizable in short periods of time.
Q. What determines whether they gain or lose?
A. A predatory female in the acquisitive mode will usually be at her thinnest. They take on a lean, hungry look. Once they've run their prey to the ground, and/or become non-acquisitive, they tend to gain weight, to lose the fighting trim.

The Invisible Man

Q. Who is the invisible man?
A. Any man the predatory female has deemed to be of no further use. Although she'll go to extremes pleasing and cultivating a man when she's in the acquisitive mode, she views him as untouchable once his purpose is served. He totally ceases to exist in every way. He becomes a nonperson and is fair game for the carrion birds of society.
Q. How can the male fall so low in her esteem?

A. He never achieved any other status. He is commonly misled through his failure to grasp the predatory nature of the female. He may have been a victim of the chameleon syndrome. Indeed, one of the biggest stumbling blocks for men, especially those reared by women, is the understanding that no woman will ever love them, particularly in the manner they desire.

Q. Why do you say that?

A. A woman's love is like a hand powered grinding wheel. If you pump furiously and wind it up, she will do the job, make noise, even throw off sparks. She will respond, but only respond. The minute you release the handle . . . she begins winding down. She can only respond in a temporary manner. That's why an adult female will rarely call you or initiate anything. They are only constructed to respond.

Q. And the invisible man?

A. He is not allowed to crank the handle. Once the charade is over, and that day comes for every man, the female has no feeling, no remorse, no conscience, and no empathy for the discarded male. He becomes the invisible man.

Mutual Exclusion

Q. What is the rule of mutual exclusion?

A. One of the few safeguards nature has

provided for those dealing with predatory females, the rule states: The more you like her, the less she'll like you, and vice versa. Although often unappreciated, nature is trying to warn those who see this rule in action. The more interest you show in a female, the less interesting you are to her. Conversely, a commitment to one will kindle the interest of others. This is because, like in the Garden of Eden, the female always wants what is denied her.

Natural Talent

Q. Do you see the predatory female as an actress?
A. When the circumstances dictate, a predatory female is capable of astounding theatrics. She can cry at will, appear emotionally devastated, throw temper tantrums, laugh, smile, charm the onlookers, rise up indignantly, take you into her confidence, become seductive, turn icy, or assume any role she deems appropriate. The talent comes involuntarily with the chameleon syndrome, but is always at her disposal.

No Free Lunch

Q. Are there any freebies at all with a predatory female?

A. Virtually none. A primary trait of the predatory female is that she deprives you of your peace of mind in direct proportion to the amount of time you spend with her. It is a natural sapping process from which there is no escape. Starting with your mind, it soon extends to your money and possessions. It's heads she wins, tails you lose. Never suppress the tingling uneasiness that accompanies the dealing with females. Nature is saying that you are the little woodchuck succumbing to the hypnotic majesty of the weaving cobra.

Doctor Doctor

Q. What is the doctor's role in the life of the predatory female?
A. Doctors are a big part of the predatory female's security. Consequently, predatory females are very doctor oriented and engage in a continuous form of doctor worship. A trait of predatory females is that they perpetually "seek to the physicians." This trait is encouraged by the matriarchal system which is the foundation of the doctor cult. The system encourages a constant barrage of doctor-idol TV serials and soap operas.
Q. How can I discern this trait in a female?
A. If you say something against doctors in general, a predatory female will likely take it as a personal insult. Also, listen carefully for

the possessive pronoun "my." It will be "my" doctor this and "my" doctor that. The reverent intimacy they use with "my doctor" contrasts interestingly with the suppressed contempt of "my husband."

The Wrangler

Q. Why is the handling of a young filly so educational where predatory females are concerned?

A. Young female horses exhibit many of the characteristics of the predatory female. If you charge wildly into the corral, she'll run away from you. If you ease into the corral, take your time, and bring something that interests her (like food), she'll become curious and wander up to sniff you out. Sudden movements will spook her. She will cost you a lot of money. She is dangerous and can hurt you. She is beautiful, unpredictable, and fun to watch. She needs constant attention. She will get into trouble if ignored. In groups, they quickly establish a pecking order since they basically don't like each other. If you let her have her own way, she'll run all over you. If she doesn't respect you, she's useless. She is capable of foundering (eating herself to death). She will often behave irrationally and can do you both great injury. Marrying her would be a huge mistake.

A Lie, Is A Lie, Is A Lie

Q. Does a predatory female ever tell the truth?

A. Only when it suits her acquisitive purposes. Where lies are concerned, the predatory female is a long ball hitter. Biblically, the first lie ever told was to a female. This female, Eve, was given personal instruction by Satan. She has never forgotten this, and her most effective technique today is the same used by Satan. After a steady progression of truths, she slips in the lie, or simply raises doubt and then *suggests* the lie. Scene: Evening in front of the fireplace.

"It's fun being together, isn't it?"

"Uh huh."

"You love all this attention, don't you?"

"Uh huh."

"Think how much nicer it would be if we were married." (Surely ye shall not die!) Aside from histrionics, the truth is not in them.

No Honor Among Thieves

Q. Do predatory females like each other?

A. Predatory females basically hate each other. Two con artists working the same street corner might be civil to accommodate business, but they'll never be sincere friends. So it is with predatory females. They are hustlers.

34

They're working a peanut shell game and the competition is rugged. They will exchange information, spy on each other, socialize, or freeze each other out. It's the law of the jungle. No one knows a predatory female like another female . . . and they don't trust each other. This basic rule is worthy of consideration.

The Scene

Q. Is the embarrassing argument or public display a characteristic of the predatory female?
A. The predatory female is capable of turning on you, in front of your friends, without the slightest compunction. An embarrassing scene doesn't bother her in the least unless you are the one causing it. Screaming, scratching, hitting, loud profanity, throwing and breaking objects, and tossing drinks are some of her favorites. Curiously, some of the worst outbreaks are between sisters. The image of two cats, fighting loudly enough to wake the neighborhood, comes to mind.

Tracks

Q. Do predatory females have distinguishing living habits?
A. Several, and here are some examples: (1) Look inside her car. Vehicles belonging to

predatory females are often littered with cigarette butts, pop cans, shoes, clothing, wrappers, hangers, old make-up containers, and other trappings of the female. Predatory females are restless spirits (they move every ten to fifteen months in the acquisitive mode) and may even live out of their cars for short periods. Further, if the car is a very expensive one, you should consider the possibility that she is a veteran predator and potentially dangerous. (2) A bedroom floor littered with the same type of debris described above. (usually done while watching TV in bed) is another track of the predatory female. The debris may include cat or dog feces. (3) Predatory females are patently lazy. They'll drive around a parking lot, forever searching out a slot next to the entrance, to avoid walking a few extra feet. They put their suitcases on little carts when traveling, despite spending more effort wrestling the carts than simply carrying the suitcases. They pull plugs out by the cords, leave the lids off containers, and refuse to read instructions or manuals accompanying technical devices or equipment.

Jaws

Q. How do predatory females compare with sharks?
A. The similarities are alarming, and indeed, sharks are almost perfect soul mates to preda-

tory females. Sharks have small brains but are masters at survival. They operate solely from instinct and are totally unpredictable. Their only purpose is self-preservation and they are completely devoid of any capacity for love. They are infinitely treacherous and have no enemies except themselves. They eat each other. They operate in packs and prey on isolated victims. They are restless and constantly on the move. A man, dealing with a predatory female, is like a man in the water with a shark. The environment (the matriarchal society) belongs to the predator. A man needs luck or special training to survive. Conditions permitting, a shark isn't satisfied with just one chunk of the victim . . . it keeps coming back for more.

Self Destruction

Q. Is there a pattern of self-destruction in the predatory female?
A. Strangely, yes. The more predatory she becomes, the more likely she is to do herself in. In the advanced stages, she becomes her own worst enemy. Sign to watch for: Lying in the sun for years until she has skin like a Komodo dragon. The basic rule states that ultimately a predatory female will defecate in her own mess kit. This extraordinary occurrence has often saved a hapless male in the eleventh hour.

The Nature Of The Beast

Q. Can a predatory female ever be re-conditioned or reformed?

A. Never. They are perpetually driven to stalk the earth, seeking whom they might devour, and you should never, repeat never, try to reform one. She'll only destroy you. Moreover, don't rebuke her for her actions. She is a slave to her predatory nature and can't help herself. Concentrate instead on appreciating her primal beauty, her hypnotic moves, dodging the bullet, and emerging unscathed from your relationship with her. Remember, she likes you for completely different reasons than you like her, and further, sex means nothing to her. She can get all she wants at the drop of a hat. An excellent reference, when discussing the nature of the beast, is Mildred Rogers from Maugham's *Of Human Bondage.* She is the quintessence of the predatory female's seductive, ruinous style. Of course, Philip Carey's attempts to rehabilitate her were completely fruitless.

> "Despite my 30 years of research into the feminine soul, I have not yet been able to answer . . . the great question that has never been answered: What does a woman want?"
>
> —*Sigmund Freud*

THE DATE AND THE LIVE IN

"Never try to impress a woman or
she'll always hold you to that standard."

– W.C. Fields

Boot Camp

Q. How do the concepts of predatory females apply to dating?

A. Dating is the females' boot camp for males. Here the man is taught to habitually finance the woman in nearly everything. He learns to be a combination chauffeur and valet while paying for the privilege. Additionally, he becomes conditioned to sitting at her feet, leash in mouth, tail wagging, anticipating the slightest hint of a sexual favor. His female drill instructor is the end product of 6000 years of survival of the fittest. While he is usually there just for fun, she's working. Even if her motives are only entertainment, she's playing hardball. If simply to make someone else jealous, she will polish her predatory skills on the date. Manipulating him is her business and he, almost never forewarned by parents or friends, is usually an amateur at defending himself. Further, a man on a date today is, by his very presence, often giving his implied consent to be used as a footstool. The matriarchy has couched these unspoken demands in the guise of customs and manners. If you refuse to perform as expected, then YOU are at fault. It's a curious parallel with the current public smoking controversy.

Q. How so?

A. Like a smoker who persists in polluting public air, forcing people to breathe waste by-products, a predatory female will consider YOU the bad guy if you won't let HER dump on YOUR head.

Q. So predatory females are dangerous, even on the dating level?

A. For the formal dater today, the hours are long and the pay is low, but SOMEBODY'S got to do it! Dating is the beginning of the cat and mouse game that women play with men. The game may extend beyond marriage. The cat will play with the mouse as long as she is amused, but when she becomes bored, she eats the mouse for lunch.

"Every woman is at heart, a rake."
—*Alexander Pope*

Slot Machine

Q. Can a man ever hope to break even with a female?

A. No. In the end, the female will always disappoint him. The slot machine rule applies at all times.

Q. What is the slot machine rule?

A. An extension of the principle that there is no such thing as a free lunch, the slot machine rule states that dealing with a woman on a personal level is like playing with a slot machine. It's fun to watch, to play with, and it gives rewards. But the odds are against you. The longer you play the same machine, the more it will cost. It will periodically pay off in small amounts, teasers, but you will invariably end up in the red.

Q. And a date is like feeding in the first quarter?

A. Yes, and you might hit a jackpot. But sooner or later the slot takes it all back with interest.

Q. What if you just quit?

A. Before you are even out of sight, the machine is being cranked by another sucker. Indeed, he was probably cranking surreptitiously before your departure.

Public Property

Q. Why do you describe predatory females as

being in the public domain?

A. The image of a man dragging a woman to his cave and sequestering her for himself is a popular fantasy. It has no application to the modern, predatory female. The entire concept of a male maintaining a female for his exclusive enjoyment is completely fictitious. This applies not only to sexual favors, but other charms as well.

Q. What import does this have in a dating situation?

A. If an individual fails to understand that a female's charms are never given, only loaned, he is doomed to exploitation. The male must constantly remember that there is absolutely no such entity as an exclusive use of a woman's sexual favors. There are always other men, and sometimes women. The man's innate desire to possess a female, to have his own little sex doll and intimate companion, is his biggest vulnerability. A predatory female will use this weakness to lead him into a trap and destroy him.

The Love Of My Life

Q. Who is this "love of my life" that women refer to?

A. The phrase applies to an imaginary man that most women feel they will someday meet. He is the one they are always searching for. He is her lover. The label is often applied to prospective husbands, but shortly after marriage is reassigned to someone else, often imaginary. Thereafter, successive lovers fill the role.

Q. So the predatory female always has two men in her life?

A. Three. We must not forget the gynecologist, a doctor she can enjoy a special intimacy with and fulfill some fantasies in the bargain.

The Gyno

Q. Would the predatory female place her gynecologist on an equal level with her husband and lover?

A. Certainly. Moreover, she will confide things in him that husbands and lovers never hear. He is the high priest to the volcano (the fountain of female magic). He enjoys a rapport with her source of power.

Q. How does this apply to a date or live-in?

A. Consider this: You've wined and dined a young lady all evening and been invited into her home. She plays soft music and kisses you, but says it's improper to have sex until she's known you longer.

Q. What's wrong with that?

A. Nothing, until the other shoe drops. The following morning she goes to her gynecologist. Although happy to wear everyday old clothes around her "loved" ones, she departs for the gyno appointment dressed to receive royalty. Arriving at the office, she is promptly ushered into the stirrups. She eagerly awaits the doctor who is a twenty eight year old suburban sex fiend wearing ten pounds of gold body jewelry. He drives a red Porsche with personalized plates saying "OB-GYN." Within moments, this stranger is practically up to his elbows in her vagina—in the interest of medicine. Basic rule: The accessibility of the female genitalia hinges strictly on her immediate, conceived objectives. So meanwhile, as the unpaid valet and volunteer batman of the previous evening, you are left with a mail order, inflatable sex doll.

Q. What about the fantasies?

A. For many predatory females, a visit to the gyno is a socially acceptable form of rape or exhibitionism. After all, it's only a question of what part of his body he puts into her. And many will state they are in love with their gynos. "He understands me. He is intimate with me, therefore we have to be close." Some even flirt with the doctor while propped in the stirrups, flanging their labia, and behaving as if nothing unusual is in progress.

Working

Q. When is a predatory female "working?"

A. The predatory female is working when she is in the process of preying on a male or another female. The males are by far the most frequent victims. A visit to any popular restaurant, for example, will enable you to see predatory females working. While the male is paying for the dinner and drinks, she is further ensconcing herself by applying feminine charms and doing little numbers on his head. She may be telling him why they should be living together, be married, whatever. She may be cultivating an all expenses paid vacation. The possibilities are endless and the predatory female knows how to exploit every advantage when she is working.

Q. What about her job or career?

A. Her job is what she does when she's not working.

Feast Or Famine

Q. Why can I go for months without meeting an interesting girl and finally, when I do meet someone, girls that ignored me suddenly become friendly?

A. A man who is alone tends to radiate a lean, hungry look that drives women away. Your new association with a woman has eliminated that deprived image and added a seasoning of decadence that attracts the female. You have become interesting to them. Further, if they perceive you as spoken for, they'll want you even more because the predatory female always wants what she can't have.

Cloak And Dagger

Q. Recently I made the disturbing discovery that, while I was in the shower, my girlfriend sneaked a look through my wallet and address book. Does that qualify her as a predatory female?

A. Does Howdy Doody have a wooden ass? Of course it does, but don't be overly alarmed. She is "working." The creatures will do this. Enjoy her performance. Incredibly, your relationship with her is probably at its zenith. This is simply a danger signal and common behavior for a predatory female who is acquisitive, seriously zeroing in on you. She considers you ripe for the plucking. It's also a sign that you have probably let the camel get its head a little too far into the tent. The predatory female never refers to these types of indiscretions as snooping. They call it "tidying up" or "cleaning."

Love And War

Q. Does the "all is fair in love and war" idea need to be reappraised?

A. Definitely. "All is fair in love and war" is an old saying that isn't taken seriously by today's men. An acquisitive female will go far beyond the bounds of propriety and good manners to achieve her goals. In her mind, almost nothing is construed as going too far. She doesn't consider it underhanded to rifle through his wallet and personal effects, to spy on him through his friends, or tell any lie that is expedient. Honesty and integrity are of no concern to a fully bloomed, predatory female in the acquisitive mode. Amazingly, she would defend her moratorium on integrity as a woman's privilege. She can be totally ruthless in this regard. The male's failure to grasp this has led to much unhappiness.

Brinksmanship

Q. What about danger in dating?
A. You could be the pawn in a scheme to make the husband or boyfriend jealous and end up being shot. You may contract a disease. She may rob you or slash her wrists in your shower. A routine traffic citation may result in your being jailed because she dropped drugs in your car. You could be in a serious traffic accident. The very fact she is with you points to both the acquisitive mode and the chameleon syndrome with all their dangers. Dating is usually the medium predatory females use to "hook" a man. The words "catch," "snare," and "trap" are also popular. These words carry a message. If marriage is the skewering and broiling of the scrotum, dating is tantamount to dangling the gonads over a fire. At its very best, dating or

living with a predatory female is brinksmanship and will exact a large toll. At its worst, you're facing possible diseases, lawsuits, physical injury, or death.

The Stinger

Q. Is there a single, dominant force used by predatory females to hypnotize and control males?

A. It is a combination of her appearance, personality, charm, wit, compatibility, and sexual prowess. Narrowed down to one thing: raw sexual allurement. Pussy power will ultimately deal the knockout blow. In the advanced stages of sexual hypnosis, the male may subconsciously want to crawl into the vagina and live there. Most normal, healthy men are capable of becoming total slaves to a well orchestrated sexual enticement and the predatory female is acutely aware of this. If necessary, she will stretch that vulva right over his head and smother him to get what she wants. But remember, although a predatory female may truly be fun and fulfilling outside of her skill in bed, this is the most dangerous type. You might let your guard down.

A Different Drum

Q. Please expound on the communication gap between the sexes.

A. Predatory females flatly think differently than males. What is black to him may be white to her. He may believe they've reached an understanding when in fact her idea of what's understood is totally different from his. Her values are different. She doesn't operate with the same set of standards, consequently there really is no common ground. Therefore, even a sincere promise or agreement is misconceived on at least one side. All treaties are faulty from the outset. Any form of contract with a predatory female is doomed to distress.

The Snake Charmer

Q. Would you characterize dating and living together as a form of snake charming?
A. Absolutely. A king cobra can reportedly rise twelve feet into the air, an awesome sight. This ancient reptile, one of the most dangerous creatures on earth, but breath taking and fascinating, makes a comparison with the predatory female unavoidable. They vary in size, some hiss before striking, others are sluggish and have to be prodded into movement, but all deserve respect.
Q. It's difficult to imagine having sex with something like that.
A. Historically, the sex drive transcends all boundaries. The man on a date must carefully

approach the wicker basket containing the snake (predatory female). He must then gently unlatch the lid and softly woo the creature while lowering his scrotum into the basket. The trick is to seduce the snake and get the lid back down before she strikes.

Q. What if they are living together?
A. A man living with his girlfriend has simply carried the snake into his bedroom. He must always be on guard and constantly insure the latch is secure on the basket.

Russian Roulette

Q. What about V.D.?
A. Venereal disease can be another one of dating's little surprises. If you plan on doing much sport fucking in our matriarchal society, you'd better wear a wet suit.

Beware Of The Camel

Q. My girlfriend has suggested that we live together. She says our relationship can't "go anywhere" otherwise. What are your views?
A. The predatory female loves to utilize the ancient Arabic principle that once a camel gets its head into the tent, getting the rest of the beast inside is easy. You not only have to consider the pandemonium and possible destruction that goes with the camel in the

tent, but the uproar and damages attendant in getting her out. Remember, there's no such thing as a free lunch. You'll pay, one way or the other, even if it's just with your peace of mind.

Snip

Q. Does the predatory female possess a subconscious desire to geld the male?

A. Yes, but usually she is happy with her head sufficiently into the tent for the legal process to perform a symbolic castration. Occasionally, however, she will show interest in less abstract methods, providing yet another reason to sleep with one eye open whenever the camel is in residence. At the very least, a man will always be weakened in proportion to the amount of time he spends with a female. They have a natural ability to drain the male, both mentally and physically. This makes him easier to control and more susceptible to her entreaties. A man living with a woman is in a most precarious position. She may wait on him until he is unaccustomed to taking care of himself. She may feed him until he becomes fat and clumsy. He loses the eye of the tiger, gradually becoming another servile gelding of the matriarchal society. The ultimate conclusion appears in the marital state where he is reduced to a legally disenfranchised figurehead, a pathetic slave of the system.

Q. Does the married man ever realize his entrapment?

A. Eventually, but many strut ignorantly and pompously around in their cages for years before awakening to their predicament. Others, to survive, adapt a "peace at any price" attitude.

Housecalls

Q. I was living alone until I became infatuated with a girl. I thought the feeling was mutual and we lived together for six months. When it became apparent she was taking advantage of my hospitality, we agreed that she would move back to her previous address, no hard feelings. Shortly thereafter, I left on a business trip. Returning home, I found the locks changed and a court order to stay off my own property, pending another hearing. It took my attorney four months to reinstate me and cost nearly ten thousand dollars. During that time I lived in a motel and she entertained wildly in my home. There was property damage, but it's evidently an uncollectible debt. Is it no longer safe to let a woman into your home?

A. Since the Lee Marvin trial it has become fashionable for women, having received some form of hospitality or "oral promise," either real or imagined, to seek financial rewards from the courts. Never has the admonition to keep the camel's head out of the tent been more timely. Allowing a woman into your home, spending the night at her place, or even lingering in her company can result in your being sued, evicted, criminally charged, subjected to public ridicule, or dragged through months of embarrassment and inconvenience. Of course, if you're married, the situation is explosive. Wives, discovering secret affairs, have been sued by their husbands' mistresses for "disruption of livelihood."

The Wasp And The Spider

Q. It's hard to realize how caring for a woman can become such a springboard to disaster.

A. There is a female wasp that can be likened to a woman. Although a tarantula spider is much bigger and stronger than this wasp, she can easily sting him until he is comatose, proceeding to build her nest on his back. She lays her eggs, raises her young, and feeds from his living body. If he resists, she stings him into lethargy again. He eventually dies, but not until she's done with him. *He simply can't ever get her off his back.* The prudent man remembers this spider whenever a female suggests living with him.

Low Down Payment

Q. My girl friend says our relationship hasn't "progressed" and if I don't let her move in, she wants to break up.
A. Undoubtedly, but keep in mind . . . they all dump you sooner or later anyway. Your only elective is choosing how far the camel's head will be into the tent when you are dumped. Have you considered minimizing your losses? This female is marketing her wares and you are reluctant to put up any front money. Why not opt for a new vendor?

The Reluctant Lamb

Q. My girlfriend and I have disagreed on living together—she wants to and I don't—but to make matters worse, her best friend encourages her to dump me.
A. Your hesitance at becoming another victim of the matriarchal system has caused you to fall into disfavor with the pack. They are pressuring your girlfriend for results and probably waving your replacement in front of her nose. They'll not be happy until the hide from your buttocks is tacked on the barn door

for drying and stretching. While your option for a clean getaway is still available, use it.

Love Gap

Q. I lived with a girl for over a year, but when I refused to marry her she broke off our affair and moved out. Within two weeks she was married to another man. I saw her recently and she behaved like a stranger, despite having professed undying love only three months previously. How do you explain such radical changes?

A. There were no changes. She never cared about you in the first place, but you have been blind to it by failing to grasp the nature of the predatory female. You loved her but she didn't love you. She is incapable of loving anyone, including her new husband. A predatory female never loves anyone but herself. Using sex to lure men into loving her, she can only pretend at loving them back. This is natural, involuntary behavior for the predatory female. She feeds them sex, fusses over them, makes them feel loved, but it's only an act. It's the chameleon syndrome in full bloom. She uses their love, or infatuation, to manipulate and control, stinging them like the wasp on the spider's back, until they are incapable of rational thought where she is concerned. The predatory female never becomes emotionally involved in the same way a male does. Her emotional involvement is strictly contingent upon her degree of success in bringing the male crashing to earth. It is not a conscious deceit, but an unconscious one. When, as in your case, she fails to trap him permanently, she can easily leave because her involvement was only temporal. This is one of the toughest axioms for men to accept: Predatory females flatly don't care. The person deserving the sympathy is the poor unfortunate who married her. He has volunteered to become the host body for this parasite, and serves as another living proof that slavery is the natural state of man.

Q. I just can't believe that women don't really ever love men, at least in the same way men love them.

A. The predatory female herself is sometimes fooled in this regard. She can be victimized by her own predatory nature, especially if she's young. But the experienced ones know better. They're counting on your inability to understand or accept it. They know your male ego will side with them. If your girlfriend sincerely believes she loves you, be sympathetic, be understanding. She just doesn't know herself yet. But don't let her immaturity bring havoc into your life.

He Who Cares Least Wins

Q. How might one enjoy dating various

attractive females without incurring some of the nightmares you've described?

A. Keep in mind the basic rule that he who cares least wins. Do not allow yourself to become emotionally attached to your dates and girlfriends, or some very unhappy days are in store for you. You may allow them to enjoy your body, your mind, and your money, but always deny them your soul.

Two Heads

Q. Doesn't the male share the blame for his demise through females?

A. He shares most of the blame. After all, he is the one with two heads, and he lets the little head tell the big head what to do.

Cheaper To Rent

Q. Given the pitfalls of associating with predatory females, perhaps prostitution should be taken more seriously.

A. Prostitutes may be the only honest women, insofar as their sex lives are concerned, because they'll generally tell you the price up front. Remember the basic rule: If it flies, floats, or fucks, it's cheaper to rent.

Isolation

Q. Since I began living with a girl, I've

noticed even my longtime friends have gradually stopped calling. Suddenly I've realized that most of "our" friends are really hers.

A. The isolation factor is another weapon used by the predatory female in her conquering of the male. She will, as the relationship progresses, begin cutting off his friends and confidants. She increasingly monopolizes his time. After awhile, his friends don't call anymore. Little by little, she becomes his only companion. This is powerful medicine because when she finally leaves him, he is totally alone. He's not only lost his only companion, but has no one to turn to.

Counseling

Q. My live-in girlfriend spends a lot of time talking with her friends about our relationship and whether we are "going anywhere." Men rarely discuss these subjects, hence I feel outnumbered and at somewhat of a disadvantage.

A. Correct. You are both outnumbered and at a disadvantage. From continuous discussion with her friends and relatives, she is probably much better prepared than you to argue whether you are "going anywhere." Since men almost never counsel each other on avoiding the snares of the predatory female, they are reduced to scrambling about individually, committing the same errors, and being singly trapped and neutralized. So effective is

58

the isolation of the males, that when one tries to counsel another he invariably gets a deaf ear. Guys just don't listen, period.

A Test

Q. My girlfriend has moved out to live with her two former roommates while I "make a decision about our future." I miss her but marriage scares me.
A. Curiously, a woman instinctively knows just how far to go in getting what she wants and rarely goes any further. Obviously the committee (or pack) is deciding your fate while you are left with nothing but a plastic Judy and a tube of Mr. Stiff.

Breaking Cover

Q. My girlfriend recently became extremely upset when I didn't leave what she considered an "appropriate" tip at a restaurant. She accused me of being cheap, and later, a tightwad. She said I "embarrassed" her. Is this an indication of a dangerous predatory female?
A. When a woman makes any kind of remark to the effect that you are stingy, remember that this is a way of declaring her expertise at spending someone else's money (probably yours).

The Blitz

Q. What is the blitz?
A. It's the heavy bombardment used by the predatory female when she is making her final move to coerce you into some arrangement favorable to her, usually marriage. Often accompanied by the ultimatum, the blitz consists mainly of a barrage of reasons why you should agree to marry her. Some examples are:

- You will end up a lonely old man.
- You won't have anyone to come home to.
- You'll never meet anyone like her again.
- Who will take care of you when you're old?
- You'll never know the joys of having children.
- Letting her go means the end of the gourmet meals.
- You won't have anyone to share your life with.
- You couldn't stand to see her with someone else.

Remember, a predatory female doesn't have to be living with you in order to subject you to the blitz.
Q. Is there anything I might do to prevent the blitz?
A. Take a calculated risk and tell her, at the earliest point in your relationship, that you

want to marry her. Propose to her on the first date. Hopefully she will reject the idea, even stare curiously at you. Never mention it again. If the subject ever resurfaces, simply say that you were turned down once and don't want to think about it anymore. It's too painful.

Reminders

Q. Are there signs to indicate a blitz may be in the offing?

A. The blitz can be detonated by many things like her best friend or sister announcing wedding plans, or the arrival of her thirtieth birthday. Specific signs may even be absent since the predatory female, like the shark, can strike without warning. However, if she starts leaving numerous personal articles in your home (clothes and toiletries), or begins practicing her signature using your last name, she is getting ready for a power move.

Q. Why would she begin leaving personal articles in my home, aside from convenience?

A. The personal articles give her a reason to come back, they remind you of her, and they drive other women away.

Collapse

Q. Why do so many guys finally just give in to the demands of these women?

A. Aside from all the entrapments and coercions discussed earlier, a lot of men just don't know what to do with themselves unless they have a woman in the background, telling them what to do. These are the terminal victims of the matriarchy. Additionally, giving up is a lot easier when everyone around you is surrendering, too. Slavery is the natural state of man.

The Ultimatum

Q. My live-in girlfriend threatens to leave me very soon if we don't get married. She says she will regretfully find another man, one who understands her needs. Since all of my friends have been ripped off, I am suspicious of marriage, but losing her would be a devastating blow to me. I have grown very comfortable with her. What do you recommend?

A. You are facing the ultimatum, the calling of your hand, the springing of the trap, and the most common power move of the predatory female. "If I don't get what I want, I'll leave and look elsewhere. I, me, I, me." This is always the bottom line with a predatory female. A man cohabits peacefully (more or less) with a woman as long as he does what she wants. If he balks at his load, she leaves him unless he has become some sort of personal challenge. In that case, she'll stick around until the matter is resolved, but will begin lining up replacements. Starting with Adam, who purposely ate the fruit (knowing full well the consequences), men have historically given in TO AVOID BEING LEFT BY THE WOMAN. Remember, if she doesn't get what she wants, she is perfectly willing to be without you. You are expendable. Will you be any less expendable after she has what she wants?

Unload the hairbag. You've already made the mistake of letting the camel into the tent. Even without marriage, you may have trouble getting her out through the door. There may be a scene. The camel may buck, collapsing the tent and strewing your belongings all over the desert. But at least you'll still own the tent and its furnishings.

You are going to have to face being alone until you find another squeeze. This may take some remedial training and conditioning. But first you must get rid of the problem. Act worried. Tell her to go ahead and move out because you need to make up your mind alone. It's a tough decision. You need a couple of months by yourself. Be accommodating and help her find new quarters. Help her move. Get your house key back. Send her change of address to the post office. Once she's out of your house, get her out of your mind and remember Lot's wife . . . don't ever look back.

Role Reversal

Q. What is the role reversal safeguard?
A. It's a simple step to guard against doing something stupid when dealing with a predatory female. Just reverse the situation and ask yourself if she would do what she's asking or expecting you to do. A good example is marriage. Few women would marry if the conditions and ground rules were reversed. Under no circumstances would a predatory female put herself in the legally and financially subservient position that a man assumes when he marries. Role reversal always illuminates dealings with predatory females. Sometime when buying an expensive dinner for a female, ask yourself if she would do that for you. Would she buy your dinner and pay for your drinks? Anytime you find yourself fanning your wallet around a woman, try the role reversal test.

Diabolical Honesty

Q. What if I resist the efforts of a predatory female and she ultimately decides her time was wasted?
A. Her feelings toward you will become sharply ambivalent. On one hand she respects you and on the other she hates you. A thwarted acquisitive female will hate you, in a nebulous, transitory fashion, and will proba-

bly say so. Often it's just "I hate you," spoken at some opportune time.

Q. But isn't there a subdued hate that women always entertain against the men they're involved with?

A. Yes, one way or the other, she'll always hate you. If she *can* control you, she'll hate you for destroying her sense of security. If she *can't* control you, she'll hate you for that. The predatory female always wants what she can't have; Satan recognized this trait in the garden. But oddly, predatory females are often honest, while they hate you, in a diabolical way. They are given to announcing their intentions, sometimes blatantly, in a style reminiscent of *Mein Kampf,* or *Das Kapital.* To hear "I'm going to get you," or "I'm going to marry you," even when you barely know them, is not unusual.

The Last Stand

Q. What if I hold my ground and refuse to marry my girlfriend, even though I'll always love her and tell her so?

A. She will shortly dump you and probably marry someone else, but she'll never forget you. Simply being "the one that got away" locks you forever into the romantic mold of her mind. She may stay with her husband, but will daydream about you. She couldn't maneuver you. You stood up for yourself, you

won, you are the hero, and that's romantic.
She'll always grudgingly admire you.

The Time Bomb

Q. My girlfriend turned thirty and immediately became demanding about a "commitment" from me. Please comment.

A. The predatory female has a short service life. The bloom comes off the rose rather quickly and they are capable of becoming panicky and demanding. Thirty is a number that lights a fuse under the predatory female. Thirty five is worse and forty is often the gateway to some psychotic behavior. The nervous, hunted look, the darting eyes, and the irrational statements coupled with ultimatums are all signs of the post thirty fuse effect. Her friends (other predatory females) have been pecking and clucking at her to get married, doing their best to make her feel inadequate. Men are generally unaware of the enormous and often vicious peer pressure that women put on each other to marry and have children. Predatory females aren't happy at simply being married themselves; they want all their friends and relatives married, too. It's time to bow gracefully out of any arrangements you may have with a predatory female of this type. Indeed, from this point forward, time is against you.

Bitter End

Q. I know when my girlfriend finally realizes
she's been dumped there will be a lot of bitterness and maybe a scene.

A. The discarded predatory female can be at
once pathetic and dangerous. If possible, you
should engineer the final departure in a public
place with good egress. Normally, predatory
females are not good losers and don't handle
rejection well. This is because they rarely have
to deal with rejection. Further, since they invariably want what they can't have, your
dumping her may only increase her desire to
"get you." In any case, be prepared for a
barrage of verbal abuse and complaints.
She'll recall her smallest dissatisfactions from
the infancy of the relationship. She may even
say you were no good from the outset, but
that she'd hoped to change you. Her friends
warned her about you and told her to dump
you a long time ago. She should have listened.
Much of what she says will approximate the
verbal rancor that marks the final hours of a
marriage.

Expensive Furs

Q. Should I mention my insights into the
character of predatory females when in the
company of same?

A. Does a chicken have lips? If you were

raising chinchillas, would you go out of your way to upset them by rattling a stick against their cages? An upset or nervous creature will produce an inferior pelt. Be nice. Don't rankle them by exposing their predatory natures. You want the most for your dating dollar and every minute with her costs money. Heckling will only detract from her performance and adversely affect the return on your investment.

Five Faces

Q. What are the five faces?
A. The ephemeral five faces of Eve are recalled by many who have experienced long relationships with predatory females. The first face appears at the introduction. Another one emerges while dating, and others present themselves while living together, marrying, and divorcing, respectively. Sometimes the faces represent five different personalities. Many divorced men are sending monthly alimony checks to women bearing little resemblance, physically or mentally, to the ones they married.

The Grovel

Q. When is the grovel appropriate?
A. Hardly ever, and only if you don't care about the outcome. Groveling, especially an

abject grovel, only drives the female away. If she senses you are doing it for fun, she may become curious, but it isn't likely to change anything.

Q. My girlfriend is seeing other men and giving me the cold shoulder when I call. She acts like a stranger and cuts the conversation short. Should I grovel?

A. Never. You are finished, so forget her. Ignore your male ego which is behind your urge to grovel. Imitate the predatory female who, being practically without ego, is almost immune from groveling. You're better off without her because, the fact is, you have indulged yourself with this woman. Indulgence is certainly permissible, but it's like an overpriced dessert in a fancy restaurant. You can pay the exorbitant charge once and still enjoy it. But if you indulge yourself twice, it's never as good the second time.

Mind And Body Control

Q. How does the predatory female manipulate your mind?

A. Although she will never say it outright, the basic rule is that you are entitled to your views as long as they agree with hers. Should a difference arise, you are out of order. But it doesn't end there. The absolute tyranny of the predatory female extends to your actions. If you do exactly what she wants you to, peace and harmony rule. But the instant you stray from the narrow path, the predatory female will jerk on the old choke chain. If you aren't married, she may find the other end empty. If you are married, you get choked.

Trial Run

Q. Is it possible to sample real marriage without the hideous commitment?
A. Fortunately, yes. Simply purchase a five hundred pound Bengal tiger and keep it in the back yard. Support it, feed it, and mount it. See for yourself if you are cut out for married life.

The Odyssey

Q. Why do you describe dating as living the Homeric epic?
A. Because as a single person, you are the modern Odysseus. You will encounter, in one form or another, Circe, Scylla, Charybdis, sirens, and lotus eaters. Like Odysseus, you may trifle with nymphs, but if you don't seek the approbation of the gods, and occasionally lash yourself to the mast, you will fall victim to the most awesome, hypnotic creature extant: The Predatory Female.

MARRIAGE

"Love is an ideal thing, marriage a real thing; a confusion of the real and the ideal never goes unpunished."

—*Goethe*

Sacrifice

Q. How does the predatory female reconcile the wedding to her overall objectives?

A. The wedding is the triumphant victory march of the predatory female and the public neutering of the groom. He, like the sacrificial victims of ancient civilizations, has even been *groomed* for the ceremony. A predatory female, being the consummate actress that she is, may actually believe in her vows, but they will soon become meaningless, rendered void by the very conditions of the contract she is locking the groom into. So we are left with nothing more than a tedious pageant where the bride, in collusion with the state, safety wires the groom's genitalia to the marital pegboard.

What You See Is Not What You Get

Q. What changes occur in the predatory female after marriage?

A. This question is answered several times in this chapter. A bride-to-be is a totally acquisitive female with her chameleon talents in full display. Her future husband will never be treated as well again. In ten years she may barely resemble the bride he remembers.

Q. How might she physically change?

A. Among the possibilities for bodily changes (some of them horrible), gaining weight seems to be very popular. A number of your larger wives can't take a step forward without drop kicking their stomachs with their knees. Fortunately for today's husbands, there are products available as anniversary or birthday gifts to the larger wife. These include cans of inner thigh grease and elastic sweat bands. The sweat bands can be worn vertically around the head and under the chin as jowl supports. Another less expensive suggestion is a box of Q tips.

Q. What are Q tips used for?

A. They are helpful during the hotter months when some wives like to lift the folds on their bellies and clean mold and other growths from the crevices. Gasoline-soaked rags are also recommended for the stubborn cases.

"A man marries hoping the woman won't change; a woman marries hoping he will change."

—Unknown

A Lifetime Haircut

Q. How is the married predatory female like Delilah?

A. The predatory female has a propensity for weakening the man. This is an ongoing occurrence in any relationship, but marriage provides an ideal setting for the gradual siphoning of his strength. A woman can cause so much needless anxiety in a man that his health suffers. He may become nervous, irritable, and develop heart trouble. Her enfeebling maneuvers provide her with a fiendish, subconscious satisfaction. The crippling effects of marriage, on men, are well known to her. A married man often acts more subdued and quiet when in the presence of his wife. She'll sap his strength, gradually wearing him down over the years in thousands of little, cumulative ways, until she's the stronger. Years of taking out the trash and picking up dog shit, among countless other indignities, finally break his spirit. The biblical account of Samson and Delilah is germane to the male versus the predatory female today. The cunning subtleties of the predatory female in the acquisitive mode are extremely dangerous, ergo Delilah cajoles Samson into revealing the secret to his strength. Later, like the man lured into marriage, Samson was unaware his strength had gone. He became a captive, was ridiculed, and finally destroyed himself.

Cat And Mouse

Q. Once having "hooked" a man into marriage, the predatory female is bored?
A. Exactly. If the cat catches the mouse, it ruins the game. Marriage is the death blow to whatever vestiges of dignity and charm the man has for her. At best, like a gelding in the corral with a brood mare, he is tolerated as long as he behaves.

Defense Of The Nest Phenomenon

Q. What is the defense of the nest phenomenon and its effects on marriage?
A. One of the most curious but poignant characteristics of the predatory female, it stems from the fact that a woman is primarily designed for reproducing the species. Her instincts are hinged to this reproductive urge. A major necessity is security. Graphically, when the female is helpless in labor and hiding in the bushes, she needs a strong male warrior to protect her and the forthcoming baby from attack or molestation. This may be the one time she must depend solely on him, independent of attorneys, girlfriends, her mother, or a side deal with another man. Naturally she requires someone who cannot be swayed from his purpose and who is strong enough to see her through the ordeal. Although a modern female may not anticipate hiding in the bushes

during labor, she still has that desire for a strong male protector. The desire is so strong that her current escort, boyfriend, or husband will find himself constantly tested. She will prod him. She will nag and jab at him to see if he will stand his ground and put her in place. If he fails to assert himself, she will feel insecure. This will provoke even more attempts to make him take charge. She wants the security that goes with her own submission. If she doesn't get it, she'll become a screeching fishwife in her primal clutching for security. She must ever be reassured that the nest will be defended.

Q. Aside from explaining the common scolds and nags, how does this phenomenon apply to marriage? How is it destructive to marriage?

A. Marriage is a poor choice for the male. The legal aspects alone are so enslaving and degrading to him that it's become a public joke. By law, a wife is in the driver's seat, period. Women know this. They know marriage is a legal and social castration of the male, and in the quasi-fantasy scenario of their minds, this disqualifies him as a defender of the nest. Samson's hair has been cut. His strength is gone. Even as the husband leaves the wedding ceremony with his new bride, she secretly knows his charisma has vanished. He has become subjugated. She looks at him with new eyes and may herself be confused as to why. The torch has passed and now their relationship is different. In her subconscious thoughts, the seed has been planted to begin looking for a new defender of the nest, regardless of how tough and protective the husband may be, and whether or not he is with her during childbirth. This seed will lie dormant until other factors cause it to germinate, but meanwhile the husband goes skipping along, unaware that he no longer meets the criteria as defender for the predatory female.

The Husband As Anti-Hero

Q. What do you mean when you say the average husband is an anti-hero?
A. For years it's been fashionable to portray the husband as a bumbling, subservient mental retard, especially in motion pictures and television. On TV sitcoms, the married man is often the subject of constant ridicule from the wife and her friends as he does one stupid thing after another. Sometimes he's a bigot, at others he's shown up by his wife or kids. The undertone is that the husband is a non-contributor, a problem, or a stumbling block. In commercials he is shown by his wife and a female real estate agent how they really can afford the new house, whereupon he goes bounding around the front yard like a moron.

Or they might show him making a total disaster of dinner on the night he is left alone with the children. The unspoken message is that when the chips are down, it's the wife or another female that knew all along what was best. Conversely, when a real hero appears, he is most often single. How would Superman, The Lone Ranger, James Bond, or even Jesus Christ have come off as a married man? The answer is: terrible. Married men are hard to sell as heroes. A picture of James Bond trying to placate a shrieking wife while she threatens to have his wages garnished doesn't fit the hero image. A married man is a cornered man. He is a man who has lost something, and this makes it hard for him to be the classic, free thinking, and independent hero.

The Contract

Q. What is marriage?
A. Marriage is a contract between three parties, traditionally a man, a woman, and the state. The state reserves the right to change the conditions and obligations of the contract without permission from the other two parties. The ingredients of the contract are fragmented into both statutory and case law. The contractual agreement with the state is rather nasty and one sided, designed to protect the female and her children. It gives her

rights to her husband's finances, property, and future earnings. It provides her with leverage to have him placed under restraining orders, evicted from his home, or subjected to garnishment of his wages. She may institute proceedings to have him committed to a mental institution. Community property laws give her rights to his retirement.

Q. What about premarital contracts?

A. We live in the "land of writs and torts." It's a society teeming with greedy attorneys who make enormous sums of money encouraging marriage (a contract) and writing additional contracts as codicils (prenuptial agreements). Attorneys are happy to sell you a premarital or prenuptial agreement, and even happier to bill you for its defense. Every married couple has a contract with the state. Some have added these additional agreements of their own. A judge may uphold or set aside provisions of the contracts as he sees fit. This is an expensive process and can be very emotional. It is not fun. A pre-marital contract may be voided if it is contrary to the public interest, written in anticipation of a divorce, or improperly constructed. Parties relinquishing something must be given consideration. That means money. At best, a pre-marital contract is a sticky wicket. Nonetheless, they are highly recommended if you are determined to involve yourself in these proceedings.

War Council

Q. Are you strongly suggesting a conference with legal counsel before marriage?
A. Absolutely. Before making large investments, most people consult outside sources and do some checking. In real estate, for example, they will get title searches and purchase insurance along with reviewing easements and zoning restrictions. But a man who gets his neck bent to marry, the biggest financial decision of his life, rarely consults anyone. He charges out and slam! He's married. Does this sound like a rational, clear thinking individual, a man with all his oars in the water? Of course not. This is another victim of the predatory female. The wasp is setting up housekeeping on the back of the host body. The camel is now completely inside the tent.

Business License

Q. Does marriage require a license?
A. Almost any dangerous act, potentially hazardous to individuals and involving the government, requires a license. Of course there is a fee. The license officially invites the state into your relationship with the bride and obligates you to a plethora of responsibilities, much of which is not understood even by

experts. This results in a tidal wave of daily litigation across the nation.

Q. Where are the licenses sold?

A. They are usually sold at courthouses because it's convenient for the state and helps familiarize you with the building that may become your second home during your divorce. More than half of the licensees return as dissolvees within a few years.

Q. Are there any requirements for the license?

A. Generally you pay the fee and present evidence of a blood test. You volunteer to become a human pin cushion for some state recognized physician. In the name of the state, he draws your blood. This ritual, reeking with symbolism, is one of the last subtle warnings to the prospective groom. It invariably goes unappreciated.

Slavery

Q. Is slavery the natural state of man?

A. History teaches that spiritual, mental, and physical slavery is the natural state of man. Freedom, like a garden, must be constantly tended. Vigilance, always the price of liberty, is highly recommended where the predatory female is concerned. Marriage is a form of slavery, even for the predatory female, and with its tricky packaging, very dangerous.

Q. Do you blame women for the ruin of millions of men through the marriage mill?

A. No. The astounding fact is that men have, of their own free wills, chosen this path to destruction. Like Adam in the Garden, they picked slavery over the prospect of being alone. They have been led en masse, by the genitals, chortling and gurgling like morons, to their own damnation. They must wear the ball and chain of holy matrimony and eventually accept that they are no longer the masters of their homes or futures. Most have little chance of ever being deprogrammed.

Guilt

Q. How does the predatory female use guilt to manipulate males?

A. Guilt is one of the predatory female's most powerful tools. With guilt, she keeps her victims on the defensive. She uses it on males from a young age, at the outset of dating, to control them. She is surprised at how eagerly they accept this charade. She makes them feel guilty about simply wanting sex, a basic, primal urge. Once successful at that, the pattern is set. Cultivating a habit of making men feel apologetic about their wants, sexual or otherwise, she assumes the aristocrat role—expecting things done for her—and silently demands that her male companion take the role of butler, chauffeur, valet, and financial benefactor. The male, while simultaneously suffering from a guilt trip and nurturing a sniveling desire to get laid, is delighted to pick up the tab. Often this process continues until she has him backed into a psychological corner where he sees his only redemption as marriage. Her acceptance of his proposal is a pardon from his guilt feelings and somehow justifies, in his confused mind, the indignities he's suffered for occasional sexual rewards. Both the predatory female and organized religion have used guilt as a method of control for thousands of years.

Self Protection

Q. What can I do to immunize myself against marriage?
A. Several things:

- Go to any pawn shop and look at all the used wedding rings for sale.
- Decide if you really want to be a guest in your own home.
- Look at the mother of your prospective bride. This could be your wife in about twenty years. Ask yourself, "Do I want to get her permission to spend my money? Do I want her to have a large claim against my retirement? Do I want to sleep with and wake-up next to this old woman?"
- Seek a neutral, disinterested individual

and try to explain to him what YOU are gaining from marriage. Think: Oh, wonderful! She has agreed to marriage. She agrees to let me support her for the rest of my life and to let my estate support her afterwards. How considerate!

- Drive to the parking lot of any large discount store selling household items. Observe what comes waddling out the door. Notice the man in the checkered shorts and jap-slaps following a large woman and three kids. He is carrying an arm load of potted plants, plumbing aids, disposable diapers, and a box of flea collars. Try and picture yourself in that role.

- Ask yourself if you really want to support any woman, and possibly some other members of her family, for the rest of your years. Contrast the joy of financially helping a friend with the possibility of being FORCED to pay, FORCED to support someone who hates you but greedily takes your money and wants more.

- Imagine selected members of her family, especially her mother, living with you for six months.

- Think about how vindictive and irrational an angry woman can be; recall that husbands may now be prosecuted for allegedly raping their own wives!

- Have your attorney lecture you for half an hour on the legal obligations and drawbacks of marriage. Consider his fee a bargain.

Marital Bigotry

Q. With the sinister facts about marriage being no secret, how can anyone deliberately go out and do that to themselves?

A. They've either been kept from knowing the truth or, upon hearing what a terrible trap marriage is, they've refused to believe it. They can't face knowing something so important to them is really a sham. They reject the truth. In addition, the matriarchal society suppresses facts about marriage so that young men will continue to eagerly offer themselves up. Newspapers will publish daily pages filled with the latest betrothals and weddings, but the divorces are either hidden back on a statistical page or left out completely. Realistically, each day's divorce settlements should be published with dollar amounts of alimony, child support, attorney's fees, and property awards.

Q. Would the matriarchal society ever allow this?

A. No. We live in a society where the predatory females, aided and encouraged by the legal system, have reduced the beauty and sanctity of marriage to the level of a mass food fight in a National Lampoon film. A daily public airing of the grim side of mar-

riage would have even our more matrimonial-
ly retarded citizens avoiding the nuptial vows.
The well would dry up. The matriarchal society would never allow this to happen.

The Family

Q. My fiancee is a terrific girl, but her family
is less than impressive. Her mother is a religious kook and her father is an alcoholic with
a stomach resembling a 150 pound sack of
chicken scratch. Should I overlook her family
in my appraisal of her?

A. You'll regret it for the rest of your life if
you do. Her family is her pedigree. They are
your window to the future, one of the few
concessions nature has given man in his bout
with the predatory female. Whatever you dislike about them, you'll someday dislike about
her, especially where the mother is concerned.
You have to ask yourself the same question
about her family that you do about her. "Are
these folks so admirable, captivating and
beautiful that it would be a credit to be sued
by them?"

The Mother-In-Law

Q. I'm always hearing about problems with
the mother-in-law. Is there really any truth to
these stories?

A. Let's put it this way. Either mother-in-law

can be a problem for wife, husband, or both. History teaches that it's the wife's mother who most often causes trouble. They meddle, criticise, and cajole. They form a secret, unholy alliance with their daughters that naturally exclude husbands. They are the smug sources of dissension in families all over the nation. Marriage is rough stuff as it is, and these old war horses increase the tension. Picture an overweight, balding woman with an increasingly apparent mustache. She is wearing a mumu, a square plastic shower cap, and has large, flabby arms spotted with bee stings (like a watermelon). She lives in a house filled with doilies, worthless gimcracks, magnetic turtles on the refrigerator door, a couple of cats, and a large ceramic goose on the front lawn. She tithes religiously, considers you a pagan, and consorts regularly with church ladies and a local minister. She's an Amway distributor and shops at K-Mart. Do you want something like that even remotely involved in your life? Also, keep in mind, daughters tend to emulate their mothers, a horrifying thought if you observe what's loose in public today.

Hurdles

Q. Can you list some points for the marriage-minded to think about and beware of *prior* to marriage?

A. Don't even give marriage the remotest consideration unless you are willing to accept:

- Being a guest in your own home
- Losing your pension
- Living with the constant threat of alimony
- Paying $75.00 for a bar of soap shaped like a frog
- Knowing that between fifty and ninety cents of every dollar you make legally belongs to your wife
- Waking up twenty five years from now with a creature that shares few if any interests with you—but controls your estate
- Knowing that your children can be taken from you at any time and used to legally extort money from you that far exceeds their support costs
- Being just another member of the vast army of subservient worker-drones in the matriarchal society
- Supporting a large cast of doctors and lawyers
- Having someone else decide how you are going to spend your money, your vacations, and your energy

The fact is, you show me a married man and I'll show you a man who's been hustled. Essentially, marriage (in America) is the handing of a rubber mallet to a selected woman, placing your balls on an anvil, and instructing her to take a swing any time she's so inclined. If you subsequently decide there is something patently one sided about the arrangement, the courts will encourage her to take numerous parting swings as you default. Further, you may be ordered to subject yourself, once per month, to other ritualistic hammerings (like sending her a large check, drawn on your account).

The Prince And The Pauper

Q. Can anyone afford marriage?
A. Two classes of individuals can afford marriage, the multi-millionaires and the indigent. The very wealthy only pay small percentages of their net worth to either keep or unload a wife. Moreover, those who aren't concerned with regular incomes aren't losing any sleep over the cost of marriage or divorce either. It's the average wage earner, the middle income worker, who gets the shaft. He pays the most to be married, and he pays the most for his divorce.

The Ceremony

Q. Does the wedding itself present any particular drawbacks?
A. It's an expensive, somewhat embarrassing ritual, often officiated by someone who barely knows the couple. Many of the participants and family members end up angry with each other. Subtle insults are traded. Inter-family

grudges germinate. Practically all the wedding gifts are for the woman. The man receives virtually nothing. This is in keeping with the practice of awarding spoils to the victor. It's also good training for the new husband who must learn to expect little. Further, any mistakes made by the husband on the wedding day will never be forgiven by the wife. She will hold the smallest faux pas against him for the rest of his days. This is also good training for the husband. He must start getting used to the idea that if something goes wrong, it's his fault.

A Wise Man

Q. Recently I attended a wedding where an interesting twist took place. As the guests presented gifts, one gave the groom a lever action rifle. The surprised groom heard the guest explain that the rifle was the only gift there for him and would be the only one he'd get out of the divorce. The bride was somewhat miffed, but her mother was quite angry. Your comment?

A. The guest was obviously experienced with predatory females, was a friend of the groom, and probably wanted to see the groom receive at least one gift.

The Afterglow

Q. What is the marriage afterglow?

A. The facial expressions of the newlyweds constitute the marriage afterglow. On the female, it is a quiet, contented, and privately triumphant look. On the new husband, it is an expression found on infants who have just crapped in their pants. He sits stupidly in an oozing euphoria, grinning from ear to ear, subconsciously knowing he's just made a serious error, but not really understanding it. He somehow suspects that now HIS clothes go on the wire hangers and HERS belong on the wooden ones.

Procreation

Q. Our society glamorizes pregnancy and childbirth. Can you give us a realistic view?
A. Be prepared to pay from three to five thousand dollars for the delivery of each child. Then brace yourself for a minimum cost of one hundred thousand dollars, per head, to raise them. These are "no frills" prices. Then, sweating profusely, you'd better throw yourself on the ground and invoke the name of God in prayer that your kids suffer no birth defects. Moreover, consider the physical destruction of your wife. Childbirth is hard on women. Their skin stretches out of proportion and their breasts sag. Some never lose the additional weight gained. Veins and bruises become permanently visible. Their hair falls out. If there are no serious complications in delivery, she may still be left with

hemorrhoids. And this is the GOOD news. The BAD news comes with odd blood types, complications in pregnancy and delivery, birth abnormalities and incompetent or careless doctors and nurses. Remember, malpractice insurance premiums haven't skyrocketed because doctors are all shining examples of professional integrity. An alarming percentage of these guys are REAL BOZOS! You should ask yourself if you want to subject your wife or girlfriend to this. Do you want to subject yourself to seeing her subjected? Do you want to spend the next twenty years raising children? Do you want to bring children into a sick and polluted world teetering on the brink of nuclear holocaust? Remember, a hell of a lot of women want to have babies, but very few want to raise children. If you commit a tort against someone, you're liable in a court of law. But a woman can methodically destroy the health of her innocent baby by smoking, by alcohol abuse, and/or drug misuse, both before and after delivery, and it's perfectly legal! Further, millions of little kids constantly take a back seat to parents' careers as fifty percent of today's mothers now work outside the home. Never in history have so many children spent most of their waking hours in the care of paid custodians, strangers for the most part, or been forced into the fearful life of a "latch key" child. Runaways are epidemic in this country. People produce children, then provide them with homes which are so terrible the kids prefer the streets! However, despite these horrors, the population continues soaring to disastrous proportions, nurtured by an army of predatory females who are driven by a consuming madness for reproduction.

The New Plebe

Q. What about the post-marriage slide into subserviency experienced by the new husband?
A. This is where the rubber meets the road. He is now the obsequious finished product of the matriarchal society. He becomes a second class citizen the very moment he is wed, and it's downhill from there. He may not comprehend his new status for a long time. Society, on the other hand, recognizes it immediately. The disenfranchised husband is part of American humor. People commonly refer to a wife as "your better half" or ask to speak with "the boss" in reference to your distaff side.

Another Pitfall

Q. What other seeds of destruction are inherent in marriage?
A. Although either unaware or able to conceal it, the new wife is almost immediately dissatisfied. She wanted stability and security,

but now finds these commodities boring. There's no adventure or excitement. She begins to chafe at the bit. She halfway wishes her husband had stuck to his guns when he originally declined to marry. She begins to resent him for marrying her. In a sense, she will never forgive him for letting her do this to herself. Finally, like a cow grazing along the edge of a field, she begins leaning on the fence. The fence bows and stretches awkwardly. Without crossing over, she may soon be able to enjoy the next pasture while defecating in her own.

The Long Shot

Q. For those of us unfortunates already married, do you have any general advice?
A. Hey, everybody gets fifty dollars of house money. Some guys go into the casino and come out wearing diamonds; others come out wearing a barrel. The odds are against you, but things just might work out. We certainly hope so. After all, a man should be entitled to spend his paycheck the way he wants.

The Submissive Wife

Q. What about the biblical concept of the submissive wife? How do you reconcile this idea with modern marriage?
A. There are those wives who attempt biblical

submissiveness and allow the man to husband his family. Unfortunately, this is simply a feeble attempt to ignore the realities of marriage. Regardless of how submissive she is, her legal position is still far superior to his, and if push should ever come to shove, she has the hammer. The marriage finally succeeds or fails on the whim of the wife. Thanks to over seventy years of female emancipation, she is in the catbird seat, period. The biblically oriented male must eventually ask himself if this inverted power structure is proper. Also, is it proper for raising children?

Little Feet

Q. I would honestly like to have children, but feel I should be married first. What about it?
A. There is rarely a man who has children in this society. He may father them, but he doesn't have them. They aren't his in the possessive sense. There are many married men who think they have children, but whose children are they, really, when the wife can almost always take them from him at any time?

Ouch!

Q. I am married, for the second time, and my wife is pressuring me to get a vasectomy reversal. She is close to thirty and feels the "biological clock" ticking.

A. The phenomena of multiple marriages has led to a demand for vasectomy reversals among older men (some already grandfathers). These martyrs illustrate the pathetic lengths men will go to please a demanding woman. You might pay a physician to say that a reversal, for you, is impossible.

Alternatives

Q. If I still want children, but realize the dangers of this endeavor in the matriarchal society, what do you suggest?

A. Try a surrogate mother. You travel overseas and make a deal with a woman to have your child for a fee. You pick a young, handsome woman and move her to a third country for the actual delivery. You pay her when the child is born and bring it home immediately afterwards. You never hear or see anything of the woman again. You then become one of the few men in this society that actually has his child.

Rejected

Q. I've been married five years and have two children. I am practically ignored around the house with the remnants of wifely attention and affection going to the children. I naturally want her to love them, but I finally understand why married men are call girls' best customers. Is there a way out?

A. There was before you married her; now you're in trouble. In varying degrees, all married men with kids must learn to accept what you're complaining of. Some kick against the goads, others go quietly, but they all acquiesce or face marital upheaval. As in other problems with wives, she has the ultimate "gotcha." You either accept what she dishes out or you can expect to get your scrotum stretched in a divorce court.

The Fall From Grace

Q. After the wedding, how does a husband verify his decommissioning, his plummet from the penthouse to the basement in the mind of his bride?

A. The magic fades. She no longer has a fervor in her eyes for him. Sex becomes a chore. She doesn't respect him or his opinions anymore. She is happy without him most of the time except when she needs some menial task performed or wants to make a major purchase. She begins reaching out for other amusements. Often, at this stage, the only impetus prolonging the marriage is a succession of diversions such as a new house, new baby, new horse, etc. The husband soon takes his place in line with the lovers (real or imaginary) and the gynecologist. The tomb is sealed.

Another Viewpoint

Q. Since, for many people, the Bible provides much of the basis for marriage, what does it say about a wife loving her husband?
A. Nowhere in the Bible is the wife ever commanded to love her husband. This is not surprising. It's a biblical principle that God doesn't ask from individuals that which they DO NOT HAVE the means to accomplish. The husband is commanded to love his wife, but she is never told to reciprocate.

Separation Of Powers

Q. Lately, while I'm at work, my wife has been spending a lot of time sipping tea with other wives in the neighborhood. Since doing this, she has gradually become more irritable and distant. Could those other wives be encouraging this?
A. Two or more females gathered together invariably result in the brewing of trouble. Groups of wives have systematically destroyed each others' marriages in communities all over the nation. Certainly one of the reasons for the relative success of marriages in the last century was the distance between homes and the difficulty of travel. Cars and telephones

have changed this and marriages have suffered. In the case of wives, idle minds really are the devil's playground. Husbands wishing to salvage something of their marriages should discourage their wives from congregating unsupervised.

Perpetual Estrangement

Q. My wife has remained distant and cold to me for a long time but has never mentioned a divorce. It's like living in a limbo. Your comments?
A. A woman doesn't have to physically leave you to dump you. Millions of wives don't give a damn about their husbands, but are happy to spend his money and enjoy, what is for them, the prestige and benefits of marriage. Indeed, predatory females are skilled at taking your money, your time, your peace of mind, and then despising you, all in a continuous cycle that may run for years.

"There is a sucker born every minute."

—*Phineas T. Barnum*

The Cowbird Syndrome

Q. Recently a friend arrived home for dinner to find his wife and children already eating and no place set for him. Upon inquiry, his wife pointed to his dinner which had been placed on the floor. Sure enough, his meal was lumped into a dog food dish next to the laundry room. He indignantly placed the dog food dish on the table and began eating his dinner. His wife immediately arose and whisked the dog food dish back to the floor. This entire performance took place in front of his children. He moved out the following day. Your comment?

A. This is a manifestation of the cowbird syndrome. The cowbird allows her mate to spend hours building a nest before she flies up to inspect. If she doesn't approve, she tears the nest apart and throws it to the ground. The mate is forced to start all over again while she sits around haughtily chirping at him. She may throw the nest down several times. If he finally pleases her, it's at the expense of most of his strength and all of his dignity. Husbands finding their belongings thrown out on the front lawn, the locks changed on their homes, or court orders forbidding their return home are all victims of the cowbird syndrome.

Q. Reverend Shannon, are you totally opposed to marriage under any circumstances?

A. I simply believe the real rules of the game should be made public, perhaps taught in school, so that everyone is made aware of the horrendous drawbacks to holy matrimony. After all, there is nothing more American, more patriotic, than a demand to give both sides a fair hearing. It's time to tear open the shutters, break down the chained doors to Castle Dracula where the marital vampire sleeps, and crack the conspiracy of silence.

Extreme Unction

Q. Why do married men often seem more desperate for sex than single men?

A. The stale relationship at home combined with a lowered self-esteem (from being trapped in a legal and financial disaster: marriage) puts his ego on the line. He therefore works very hard to get laid. Women may prefer a married man because he will snivel and cater more than a single one, at least in the short run. Eventually, however, she will begin to sandpaper the end of his peepee and the "M" word will come up, giving him a decision to make. Either way, he gets his balls whacked with a brickbat. Being married is like having your foot caught in a bear trap: You must saw off the foot; the longer you wait, the higher up your leg you must saw.

DIVORCE

"I am a good housekeeper. Whenever I leave a man, I keep his house."

—*Zsa Zsa Gabor*

Taps

Q. Can you list some indications of an impending divorce?

A. Here are some of the more common ones:

- You return home to find your clothes on the front lawn. It is raining.
- One or more of her girlfriends are always around the house.
- She behaves like a stranger, remains distant.
- The sex becomes poor to nonexistent.
- When you answer the phone, the caller frequently hangs up.
- She no longer cleans the house or the kitchen. The place is a mess.
- She wants to take the kids and visit relatives for extended periods of time.
- She disappears overnight without telling you beforehand.
- She doesn't want you to pick up the mail.

- She never goes to bed with you. She stays up late watching television by herself.
- A process server surprises you at work with divorce papers.

The Season

Q. Is there a season for divorces?
A. The predatory female can generally engineer your divorce to begin at a time most convenient for her. The summer months are popular because the kids are out of school, its easier for you to move out, and there are fewer holidays to cause regrets or second thoughts.

Playback Mode

Q. What is the playback mode of the predatory female?
A. During the final hours of your marriage, the predatory female reviles you over all the real or imaginary affronts she has held you accountable for over the years. You will be chastised for even the most insignificant or questionable slights, some you can't remember, dating back prior to the wedding. She may exhibit genuine hatred as she berates you for what she has "had to put up with." The predatory female works hard to preserve all these self-defined offenses and ceremoniously dumps them on you as the marriage collapses.

She often stages these scenes in front of your neighbors, friends, and children.

A No No

Q. What about arguing in front of the children?

A. Never, repeat never, allow this to happen. Although the predatory female is unconcerned if you come out of the bedroom, after a heated argument, to find your kids huddled against the door, crying, the scene may haunt you for a lifetime. Your impending forced move away from your children will be bad enough without that.

Nightmares

Q. My wife and I have agreed on an amicable divorce to avoid customary fighting and bitterness. Shouldn't more people consider doing it that way?

A. The term "amicable divorce" can be totally misleading. The states of divorce and amicability are mutually exclusive. A divorce is only "amicable" if the predatory female is getting exactly what she wants or what her attorney says she's "entitled" to. You should prepare yourself for some terrible experiences in the course of a divorce, especially if children are involved. You are about to see the cold side of your spouse, a primal, hissing, bone chilling transformation that is rooted in thousands of years of female survival. Brace yourself for scenes at airports where your children are torn away from you, screaming and crying, while your former spouse stands in the background with a smug, victorious sneer. Be ready for phone calls from the airline telling you that your kids' mother never showed up to meet them at the other end. Don't be alarmed when your children are allowed to "visit" you and they talk about their "other daddy." Learn to be calm when the sheriff, interrupting one of your few days with your kids, comes to your front door with "orders to show cause" why you shouldn't be paying your ex-spouse even more money than you already are. She and her boyfriend probably need new stereo equipment. Indeed, every time you see your kids, thoughts of being sued will pass through your mind. This is normal. As you begin your divorce, understand that your wife is capable of saying or doing anything against you, or your children, to get what she wants.

The Living Dead

Q. How long is the divorce process?
A. Depending on the locality, it may run from a few days to several years. Many factors tend to prolong the torturous experience. Your spouse and all the attorneys, descending upon your estate like vultures, may separately drag their feet while reaching for larger shares

of the proceeds. A dissolving marriage, like a vampire, doesn't quite die. For years, while you continue to write monthly support checks, the spectre of future lawsuits hangs over your head like a sword. Your promotions and salary increases are often followed by a visit from the process server. Also, your ex-wife's many problems have a way of ending up on your doorstep, sometimes through your children.

Mr. Nice Guy

Q. What is the basic rule to remember during a divorce?
A. No more Mr. Nice Guy. If you disregard this rule when divorcing a predatory female, she'll interpret it as weakness and not only skin you alive initially, but return, maybe years later, for another piece of your hide.

Bobbing And Weaving

Q. Can anything be done to frustrate the process server?
A. Very little. If you hold a regular job and participate in the functions of society, you'll eventually be served. It's sometimes advisable to authorize your attorney to accept service, as process servers often employ devious or illegal means in accomplishing their task. Moreover, at this stage of your marital expe-

rience, the jaws of jurisprudence have already closed upon your genitals, encouraging humble submission. Your only remaining option is to take the least painful way out.

Instruments Of Surrender

Q. What will I receive from the process server?

A. He will either hand or throw you a bundle of legal forms, some examples of which are reproduced on the following pages. They represent a joint public announcement by a predatory female and the matriarchal society of your impending trial, sentencing, and overall humiliation. That you will be found "guilty" is never in question. From this point on, you should expect to be treated much like a criminal. Your friends and neighbors will begin avoiding you. You may be ordered to stay away from your home and the immediate community. There may be a motion to order you examined by a psychiatrist—naturally at your expense. A court appointed accountant may arrive at your place of work to examine the company books, your payroll records, and possibly even your personal banking records. A new feeling invades your body, the deep down gut sense of being a fugitive. You are restrained from seeing your own children at other than specified times. Marriage assumes a new meaning to you. The following legal forms are provided as further introduction to divorce, a growth industry. Although from California, they are representative of most states. Look them over; digest their message. Imagine the joy of having to fill out the Income & Expense Declaration, maybe several times! You might see these forms, or similar ones, repeatedly over the years—even after your divorce is final—if your wife decides (like thousands of others) to sue for more money.

Big Wedding

Q. My ex-inlaws couldn't get into a pay toilet so my parents paid for most of a large and expensive wedding. With the divorce in progress, they feel ripped off, too.

A. Very common. Another basic rule states that the length of the marriage is inversely proportional to the cost of the wedding.

ATTORNEY OR PARTY WITHOUT ATTORNEY *(Name and Address):*	TELEPHONE NO.:	FOR COURT USE ONLY

ATTORNEY FOR *(Name):*

SUPERIOR COURT OF CALIFORNIA, COUNTY OF

STREET ADDRESS:

MAILING ADDRESS:

CITY AND ZIP CODE:

BRANCH NAME:

MARRIAGE OF

PETITIONER:

RESPONDENT:

PETITION FOR	CASE NUMBER:
☐ **Dissolution of Marriage** ☐ **And Declaration Under Uniform Child** ☐ **Legal Separation** **Custody Jurisdiction Act** ☐ **Nullity of Marriage**	

1. RESIDENCE (Dissolution only) ☐ Petitioner ☐ Respondent has been a resident of this state for at least six months and of this county for at least three months immediately preceding the filing of this Petition for Dissolution.

2. STATISTICAL FACTS   a. Date of marriage: c. Period between marriage and separation
                           b. Date of separation: Years: Months:

3. DECLARATION REGARDING MINOR CHILDREN OF THIS MARRIAGE
    a. ☐ There are no minor children.
    b. ☐ The minor children are:

Name	Birthdate	Age	Sex

    c. IF THERE ARE MINOR CHILDREN, COMPLETE EITHER (1) *or* (2)
       (1) ☐ Each child named in 3b is presently living with ☐ petitioner ☐ respondent
            at *(address):*

            and during the last five years has lived in no state other than California and with no person other than petitioner or respondent or both.

            Petitioner has not participated in any capacity in any litigation or proceeding in any state concerning custody of any minor child of this marriage.

            Petitioner has no information of any pending custody proceeding or of any person not a party to this proceeding who has physical custody or claims to have custody or visitation rights concerning any minor child of this marriage.

       (2) ☐ A completed Declaration Under Uniform Custody of Minors Act is attached.

4. ☐ Petitioner requests confirmation of the following as separate assets and obligations:
    Item   Confirm to

(Continued on reverse)

Form Adopted by Rule 1281
Judicial Council of California
1281 [Rev. January 1, 1983]

PETITION
(FAMILY LAW)

2710-40

MARRIAGE OF (last name—first names of parties):	CASE NUMBER:

PETITION (FAMILY LAW)

1281 (Rev. January 1, 1983)
Page two

5. DECLARATION REGARDING COMMUNITY AND QUASI-COMMUNITY ASSETS AND OBLIGATIONS AS PRESENTLY KNOWN

   a. ☐ There are no such assets or obligations subject to disposition by the court in this proceeding.

   b. ☐ All such assets and obligations have been disposed of by written agreement.

   c. ☐ All such assets and obligations are listed in the property declaration to be filed with this petition.

   d. ☐ All such assets and obligations are listed below:

6. Petitioner requests

   a. ☐ Dissolution of the marriage based on
      (1) ☐ irreconcilable differences. CC 4506(1)
      (2) ☐ incurable insanity. CC 4506(2)

   b. ☐ Legal separation of the parties based on
      (1) ☐ irreconcilable differences. CC 4506(1)
      (2) ☐ incurable insanity. CC 4506(2)

   c. ☐ Nullity of void marriage based on
      (1) ☐ incestuous marriage. CC 4400
      (2) ☐ bigamous marriage. CC 4401

   d. ☐ Nullity of voidable marriage based on
      (1) ☐ petitioner's age at time of marriage. CC 4425(a)
      (2) ☐ prior existing marriage. CC 4425(b)
      (3) ☐ unsound mind. CC 4425(c)
      (4) ☐ fraud. CC 4425(d)
      (5) ☐ force. CC 4425(e)
      (6) ☐ physical incapacity. CC 4425(f)

7. Petitioner requests that the court grant the relief or judgment specified in item 6, make injunctive and other orders as may be proper, and that

   a. ☐ Child custody be awarded
      (1) Legal custody
         (a) ☐ Joint to petitioner and respondent
         (b) ☐ Sole to ☐ petitioner ☐ respondent ☐ other (specify):
      (2) Physical custody
         (a) ☐ Joint to petitioner and respondent
         (b) ☐ Sole to ☐ petitioner ☐ respondent ☐ other (specify):

   b. ☐ Child visitation rights be granted (specify):

   c. ☐ Child support be awarded ☐ petitioner ☐ respondent

   d. ☐ Spousal support be awarded ☐ petitioner ☐ respondent

   e. ☐ Property rights be determined.

   f. ☐ Attorney's fees and costs be awarded ☐ petitioner ☐ respondent

   g. ☐ Wife's former name be restored (specify):

I declare under penalty of perjury under the laws of the State of California that the foregoing is true and correct and that this declaration is executed on (date):

_____
(SIGNATURE OF PETITIONER)

....
(TYPE OR PRINT NAME OF ATTORNEY)

_____
(SIGNATURE OF ATTORNEY FOR PETITIONER)

ATTORNEY OR PART WITHOUT ATTORNEY *(Name and Address):*	TELEPHONE NO.	FOR COURT USE ONLY

ATTORNEY FOR *(Name)*

SUPERIOR COURT OF CALIFORNIA, COUNTY OF

STREET ADDRESS

MAILING ADDRESS

CITY AND ZIP CODE

BRANCH NAME

PETITIONER/PLAINTIFF:

RESPONDENT/DEFENDANT:

INCOME AND EXPENSE DECLARATION	CASE NUMBER:

Step 1 **Attachments to** **this summary**	I have attached completed Income Information and Expense Information forms. *You must complete and attach the expense information and income information forms.*
Step 2 **Answer all** **questions that** **apply to you**	1. Are you receiving or have you applied for or do you intend to apply for welfare or AFDC? ☐ Receiving ☐ Applied for ☐ Intend to apply for ☐ No. 2. What is your date of birth (month/day/year)?. . . . . _____ 3. What is your occupation? _____

4. Mark the highest year of education completed:

		Primary			High School	College	Postgraduate
		1 2 3 4 5 6 7 8			9 10 11 12	13 14 15 16	17 18 19 20

5. Are you presently employed? ☐ Yes ☐ No
   a. If yes: (1) Where do you work? (name and address): _____
                (2) When did you start work there (month/year)? . . . . _____
   b. If no: (1) When did you last work (month/year)?. . . . . _____
                (2) What were your gross monthly earnings? . . . . _____
6. What is your social security number: __ __ __ - __ __ - __ __ __ __
7. What is the total number of minor children you are legally obligated to support? . . . . _____

Step 3 **Monthly income** **information**	8. Total gross monthly income (from line 4 of Income Information): . . . . $ _____ 9. Total monthly deductions (from line 12 of Income Information): . . . . $ _____ 10. Net monthly disposable income (from line 13 of Income Information): . . . . $ _____

Step 4
Deductions and
adjustments
	11. ☐ Hardship deductions are requested in the total amount of: . . . . $ _____
	     (See item 21 of Expense Information)
	12. ☐ Each parent has physical custody more than 30% of a 365-day period.
	     (See item 22 of Expense Declaration)

Step 5 **Expense** **information**	13. Total monthly expenses from line 17 of Expense Information: . . . . $ _____ 14. Amount of these expenses paid by others: . . . . $ _____
Step 6 Other **party's income**	15. My estimate of the other party's gross monthly income is: ☐ unknown . . . . $ _____
Step 7 **Date and** **sign this form**	I declare under penalty of perjury under the laws of the State of California that the foregoing and the attached information forms are true and correct. Date:

▶

. . . .
(TYPE OR PRINT NAME OF DECLARANT)

                   (SIGNATURE OF)
☐ Petitioner   ☐ Respondent

Form Adopted by Rule 1285.50
Judicial Council of California
1285.50 (Rev. July 1, 1985)

INCOME AND EXPENSE DECLARATION
(Family Law)

Civil Code, § 4721

Step 1 Figure your total gross annual income *If your income is irregular, show the total for the past 12 months and indicate that your income is irregular*	1. Total gross salary or wages, including commissions, bonuses, and overtime paid during last 12 months:	1. $ _____
	2. All other money received during last 12 months **except welfare, AFDC, spousal support from this marriage, or any child support.** *Specify sources below:*	2a. $ _____
	Include pensions, social security, disability, unemployment, military basic allowance for quarters (BAQ), spousal support from a different marriage, dividends, interest or royalty, trust income, and annuities.	2b. $ _____
		2c. $ _____
	Include income from a business and rental properties. Prepare and attach a schedule showing gross receipts less cash expenses for each business or rental property.	2d. $ _____
	3. Add lines 1 through 2d	3. $
Step 2 Figure your gross monthly income	4. Divide the amount on line 3 by 12 months **total gross monthly income**	4. $
Step 3 Figure the deductions from income each month	5. State income tax withheld:	5. $ _____
	6. Federal income tax withheld: . . . . a. Number of exemptions claimed on W-4 form: _____ b. Number of exemptions claimed on last federal income tax return: _____	6. $ _____
	7. FICA *(Social Security)* or self employment tax or an amount not greater for persons not subject to FICA, if the amount is used to secure retirement or **disability benefits:**	7. $ _____
	8. Health insurance:	8. $ _____
	9. Mandatory union dues:	9. $ _____
	10. Mandatory retirement and pension fund contributions: . . . . *Do not include any deduction claimed in item 7.*	10. $ _____
	11. Court ordered child or spousal support **actually being paid** for a relationship other than that involved in this proceeding:	11. $ _____
	12. Add lines 5 through 11 **total monthly deductions**	12. $
Step 4 Net disposable income	13. Subtract line 12 from line 4 **net monthly disposable income**	13. $
Step 5 Other income and deduction information	14. Current gross monthly salary or wages:	14. $ _____
	15. AFDC, welfare, spousal support from this marriage and child support from other relationships received each month:	15. $ _____
	16. State disability insurance withheld each month:	16. $ _____
	17. Monthly costs of child care to permit your work or education:	17. $ _____
Step 6 Other property owned	18. Cash & checking accounts:	18. $ _____
	19. Savings & credit union accounts:	19. $ _____
	20. Stocks, bonds, cash value of life insurance, other liquid assets:	20. $ _____
	21. All other property, real or personal *(specify below):*	21. $ _____

Form Adopted by Rule 1285.50a
Judicial Council of California
1285.50a [New July 1, 1985]

INCOME INFORMATION
(Family Law)

Civil Code, § 4721

PETITIONER/PLAINTIFF:	CASE NUMBER:
RESPONDENT/DEFENDANT:	
EXPENSE INFORMATION OF *(name)*:	

1.

a. List all persons living in your home **whose expenses are included below** and their income: ☐ Continued on attachment 1a.	name 1. 2. 3. 4.	age	relationship	gross monthly income
b. List all other persons living in your home and their income: ☐ Continued on attachment 1b.	1. 2. 3.			

MONTHLY EXPENSES

2. Residence payments

    a. Rent or mortgage . . . . $ _____

    b. Taxes & insurance . . . . $ _____

    c. Maintenance . . . . $ _____

3. Food at home . . . . $ _____

4. Food eating out . . . . $ _____

5. Utilities . . . . $ _____

6. Telephone . . . . $ _____

7. Laundry & cleaning . . . . $ _____

8. Clothing . . . . $ _____

9. Medical & dental . . . . $ _____

10. Insurance *(life, accident, etc. Do not include auto, home, or health insurance)* $ _____

11. Household supplies . . . . $ _____

12. Education *(specify)*:

    $ _____

13. Entertainment . . . . $ _____

14. Transportation & auto expenses (insurance, gas, oil, repair) . . . . $ _____

15. Installment payments (insert total and itemize below at 18) . . . . $ _____

16. Other *(specify)*:

    $ _____

17. TOTAL MONTHLY EXPENSES . . . . $ _____

18. ITEMIZATION OF INSTALLMENT PAYMENTS OR OTHER DEBTS   ☐ Continued on Attachment 18.

CREDITOR'S NAME	PAYMENT FOR	MONTHLY PAYMENT	BALANCE	DATE LAST PAYMENT MADE

19. ATTORNEY FEES

    a. I have paid my attorney for fees and costs: $ _____   The source of this money was:

    b. I have incurred to date the following fees and costs:

    c. My arrangement for attorney fees and costs is:

    d. ☐ Attorney fees have been requested.

    I confirm this information and arrangement. . . . _____

                                             (SIGNATURE OF ATTORNEY)

. . . .
(TYPE OR PRINT NAME OF ATTORNEY)

(Continued on reverse)

Form Adopted by Rule 1285.50b
Judicial Council of California
1285.50b [New July 1, 1985]

EXPENSE INFORMATION
(Family Law)

Civil Code, § 4721

PETITIONER/PLAINTIFF:	CASE NUMBER:
RESPONDENT/DEFENDANT:	
EXPENSE INFORMATION OF *(name)*:	

This question must be completed if there are minor children

20. Health insurance for my children ☐ is ☐ is not available through my employer.
Monthly cost paid by me for the health insurance for the children only is $ . . . .
Do not include the amount paid or payable by your employer or others.

Complete section 21 if you claim expenses that have caused extreme financial hardship. Enter them here, check item 11 on the Income and Expense Declaration, and enter total on line 11 of that form

21. ☐ The court is requested to allow the deductions identified below, which are justifiable expenses that have caused an extreme financial hardship.

	Amount paid per month	How many months will you need to make these payments
a. ☐ Extraordinary health care expenses *(specify and attach any supporting documents)*:	$	. . . .
b. ☐ Uninsured catastrophic losses *(specify and attach supporting documents)*:	$	. . . .
c. ☐ Minimum basic living expenses of dependent minor children from other marriages or relationships *(specify names and ages of these children)*:	$	. . . .
d. ☐ Other *(specify and attach supporting documents)*:	$	. . . .
e. Total hardship deductions requested *(add lines a-d)*:	$	

Complete this section if there are minor children of this relationship

22. The physical custody of the children will be shared in the following manner during a 365-day period:

Child's Name	Petitioner/Plaintiff number of days	Respondent/Defendant number of days	Is child on AFDC? Yes No
a.			☐ ☐
b.			☐ ☐
c.			☐ ☐
d.			☐ ☐

If each parent has physical custody of any of the children 110 days or more, check item 12 on the Income and Expense Declaration.

1285.50b [New July 1, 1985]

EXPENSE INFORMATION
(Family Law)

Page two

MARRIAGE OF (last name—first names of parties)	CASE NUMBER:

APPLICATION FOR ORDER AND SUPPORTING DECLARATION OF ☐ **PETITIONER** ☐ **RESPONDENT**
☐ **CLAIMANT** requests the following relief.

1. ☐ **CHILD CUSTODY**
   a. **Child**
      (1) Name   (2) Age

   b. Request custody to

   ☐ **TO BE ORDERED PENDING THE HEARING**
   c. ☐ Modify existing order
      (1) filed on (date):
      (2) ordering (specify):

2. ☐ **CHILD VISITATION**
   a. ☐ Reasonable
   b. ☐ Other (specify):

   ☐ **TO BE ORDERED PENDING THE HEARING**
   c. ☐ Modify existing order
      (1) filed on (date):
      (2) ordering (specify):

3. ☐ **CHILD SUPPORT**
   a. **Child**
      (1) Name   (2) Age

   b. Support requested
      (1) Monthly amount
         $

   c. ☐ Modify existing order
      (1) filed on (date):
      (2) ordering (specify):
         $

4. ☐ **SPOUSAL SUPPORT**
   a. ☐ Amount requested (monthly): $
   c. ☐ Terminate existing order
      (1) filed on (date):
      (2) ordering (specify):

   b. ☐ Modify existing order
      (1) filed on (date):
      (2) ordering (specify):

5. ☐ **ATTORNEY FEES AND COSTS**
   a. ☐ Fees: $
   b. ☐ Costs: $

6. ☐ **RESIDENCE EXCLUSION AND RELATED ORDERS**   ☐ **TO BE ORDERED PENDING THE HEARING**
   ☐ Petitioner ☐ Respondent must move out and must not return to the family dwelling at (address):

   ☐ Taking only clothing and personal effects needed until the hearing.

7. ☐ **STAY AWAY ORDERS**   ☐ **TO BE ORDERED PENDING THE HEARING**
   ☐ Petitioner ☐ Respondent must stay at least . . . . .yards away from the following places:
   a. ☐ applicant's residence (address optional):
   b. ☐ applicant's place of work (address optional):
   c. ☐ the children's school (address optional):
   d. ☐ other (specify):

8. ☐ **RESTRAINT ON PERSONAL CONDUCT**   ☐ **TO BE ORDERED PENDING THE HEARING**
   a. ☐ Petitioner ☐ Respondent shall not contact, molest, attack, strike, threaten, sexually assault, batter, telephone or otherwise disturb my peace
      ☐ and the following family or household members (name):

(Continued on reverse)

Form Adopted by Rule 1285.20
Judicial Council of California
Revised Effective January 1, 1981

**APPLICATION FOR ORDER
AND SUPPORTING DECLARATION
(FAMILY LAW)**

Civil Code
Section 4359

APPLICATION FOR ORDER AND SUPPORTING DECLARATION (FAMILY LAW)

9. ☐ PROPERTY RESTRAINT ☐ TO BE ORDERED PENDING THE HEARING
    a. ☐ Petitioner
    b. ☐ Respondent
    c. ☐ Claimant

                be restrained from transferring, encumbering, hypothecating, concealing or in any way disposing of any property, real or personal, whether community, quasi-community, or separate, except in the usual course of business or for the necessities of life.

                ☐ and applicant be notified of any proposed extraordinary expenditures and an accounting of such be made to the court.

10. ☐ PROPERTY CONTROL ☐ TO BE ORDERED PENDING THE HEARING
    a. ☐ Petitioner ☐ Respondent be given the exclusive temporary use, possession and control of the following property we own or are buying:

    b. ☐ Petitioner ☐ Respondent be ordered to make the following payments on liens and encumbrances coming due while the order is in effect:

Debt	Amount of Payment	Pay To

11. ☐ LAW ENFORCEMENT AGENCIES
I request that copies of orders be given to the following law enforcement agencies having jurisdiction over the locations where violence is likely to occur:

Law Enforcement Agency	Address

12. ☐ OTHER RELIEF (specify):

13. ☐ Facts in support of relief requested and change of circumstances for any modification are (specify):
    ☐ contained in the attached declaration

I declare under penalty of perjury under the laws of the State of California that the foregoing, including any attachment, is true and correct and that this declaration is executed on (date):. . . . . at (place): . . . .

. . . .   _____
       (Type or print name)   (Signature of applicant)

2710-180

MARRIAGE OF *(last name—first name of parties):*	CASE NUMBER:

TEMPORARY RESTRAINING ORDERS
(FAMILY LAW ATTACHMENT)

THESE ORDERS SHALL EXPIRE AT THE DATE AND TIME OF THE COURT HEARING UNLESS EXTENDED BY THE COURT.

1. ☐ RESTRAINT ON PERSONAL CONDUCT
   ☐ Petitioner ☐ Respondent   shall not contact, molest, attack, strike, threaten, sexually assault, batter, telephone, or otherwise disturb the peace of *(name):*
   ☐ and the following family or household members *(name):*

2. ☐ RESIDENCE EXCLUSION AND RELATED ORDERS
   ☐ Petitioner ☐ Respondent   must move out and must not return to the family dwelling at *(address):*

   ☐ Taking only clothing and personal effects needed until the hearing.

3. ☐ STAY-AWAY ORDERS
   ☐ Petitioner ☐ Respondent   must stay at least . . . . yards away from the following places:
   a. ☐ Residence of *(name):*
      (address optional):
   b. ☐ Place of work of *(name):*
      (address optional):
   c. ☐ The children's school *(address optional):*

   d. ☐ Other *(specify):*

4. ☐ PROPERTY RESTRAINT
   a. ☐ Petitioner   is restrained from transferring, encumbering, hypothecating, concealing, or in any way
   b. ☐ Respondent   disposing of any property, real or personal, whether community, quasi-community, or
   c. ☐ Claimant   separate, except in the usual course of business or for the necessities of life.
      ☐ and applicant is to be notified of any proposed extraordinary expenditures and an accounting of such be made to the court.

5. ☐ PROPERTY CONTROL
   a. ☐ Petitioner ☐ Respondent   is given the exclusive temporary use, possession and control of the following property the parties own or are buying:

   b. ☐ Petitioner ☐ Respondent   is ordered to make the following payments on liens and encumbrances coming due while the order is in effect:

Debt	Amount of Payment	Pay To

VIOLATION OF THIS TEMPORARY RESTRAINING ORDER IS A MISDEMEANOR, PUNISHABLE BY A $1000 FINE, SIX MONTHS IN JAIL, OR BOTH. THIS ORDER SHALL BE ENFORCED BY ALL LAW ENFORCEMENT OFFICERS.

(Continued on reverse)

Form Adopted by Rule 1285.05
Judicial Council of California
1285.05 (Rev. January 1, 1985)

TEMPORARY RESTRAINING ORDERS
(FAMILY LAW)

2710–225

MARRIAGE OF *(last name—first name of parties):*	CASE NUMBER:

TEMPORARY RESTRAINING ORDERS
(FAMILY LAW)

6. ☐ **MINOR CHILDREN**
☐ Petitioner ☐ Respondent shall not remove the minor children
☐ from the State of California
☐ other *(specify)*

7. ☐ By the close of business on the date of this order a copy of this order and any Proof of Service shall be delivered to the law enforcement agencies listed below as follows:
☐ the applicant shall deliver.
☐ the applicant's attorney shall deliver.
☐ the clerk of the court shall mail.

<u>Law Enforcement Agency</u>   <u>Address</u>

8. ☐ **OTHER ORDERS**

9. This order is effective when made. The law enforcement agency shall enforce it immediately upon receipt. It is enforceable anywhere in California by any law enforcement agency that has received the order or is shown a copy of the order. If proof of service on the restrained person has not been received, the law enforcement agency shall advise the restrained person of the terms of the order and shall enforce it.

Dated: ▶

_____
JUDGE OF THE SUPERIOR COURT

CLERK'S CERTIFICATE OF MAILING

I certify that I am not a party to this cause and that a copy of the foregoing was mailed first class, postage prepaid, in a sealed envelope addressed as shown in item 7, and that the mailing of the foregoing and execution of this certificate occurred at *(place):* California,

on *(date):*   Clerk, by _____ , Deputy

The Circus

Q. What is the atmosphere at the divorce court?

A. Inside the courtroom reigns a quiet solemnity of judgement day. But in the court lobby, a different scene prevails. There gather the supporters and spectators loyal to the predatory female. Whereas the husband is usually present with only his attorney and is understandably in a somber mood, the wife's viewpoint is entirely different. She's there to claim the spoils of victory. For her, it's a party atmosphere and she wants her friends and relatives to share the good cheer. They stand in the hallways, joking and laughing, hushing momentarily if the husband walks by. Appropriately, the bailiff should distribute party favors to the predatory female and her entourage, little pointed hats, horns, and whistles that roll out.

The Stretching

Q. What happens inside the courtroom?

A. In the course of issuing a divorce decree, the judge must decide on the size of the financial awards to the wife, order custody of the children, and divide up the property in various proportions. The following synopsis is a general summary of what usually occurs.

Spousal Support

This is alimony, one of the more pernicious
aspects of divorce. The longer you've been
married, the more you'll pay. Awards up to
one third of the husband's take-home pay are
not unusual. In some jurisdictions, women
married over twenty years are presumed to deserve spousal support for the rest of their
lives. Spousal support can be, but is not
always, tax deductible. If you fail to pay, you
can be subject to arrest in addition to having
your wages garnished.

Child Custody

Odds still largely favor the wife being awarded custody of the children unless she is proven
to be a detriment to them, an unfit mother.
It's an uphill battle for a man seeking custody
of his children, but can be easier if the wife
doesn't want her children or is confined to a
jail or mental institution.

Child Support

The dollar figure is determined by the husband's income and number of children. It's
not tax deductible for the payer. The husband
is normally ordered to pay year around, regardless of the children's visits with him. The
courts are generally agreeable to periodic increases in support, and will probably even

award attorney's fees to the ex-wife returning to court for more money. Failure to pay regularly and on time can result in arrest and criminal charges in addition to wage garnishment or seizure of property. Nationwide crime computers are now being used to track delinquent husbands.

Property Settlement

In community property states, all community property is theoretically split evenly. Bargaining for reduced spousal support (alimony), or attempts to save the husband's retirement, however, often result in grossly uneven divisions favoring the wife. Furthermore, attorneys are practiced at having previously sacred separate property judged as "donated" to the community. In states without community property laws, wives can by awarded nearly all the property. An innovation in this area is the awarding of what amounts to one half of the husband's college or professional degree to the spouse. This entitles her to half of all proceeds from the practice or use of the degree. In the case of a physician husband, for example, she would receive half of present and future earnings from his practice.

Retirement

Retirement funds accumulated after the wedding are up for grabs like other property. The longer you are married, the more jeopardized your retirement is, and the larger amount your spouse will claim. Divorcing retirees are forced to pay support (spousal and child) from the residue of their retirement.

Attorney's Fees

The husband is almost universally ordered to pay his wife's attorney's fees as well as his own. Years later, if she decides to sue him again, the rule still applies. Fees for these actions may run into thousands of dollars.

Garnishment

Wages may be garnished and property seized to pay alimony, child support, attorney's fees, or whatever else the court deems appropriate, including court costs.

The A Frame

Q. What is the A frame?
A. Near the end of the court proceedings, the judge will motion for a bailiff to wheel in the A frame. This medieval device, also known as a scrotum stretcher, aids the husband in understanding his divorce decree. The menacing machine can be rolled across the floor on its

wooden wheels. Almost unheard of prior to the emancipation of women, these A frames, or scrotum stretchers, are now standard fixtures in every divorce court. Older A frames are heavy, cumbersome, and of no interest to collectors unless they are one of the rare, antique models designed originally as labia stretchers. Only ten labia stretchers, all over eighty years old, are known to have survived. One sold recently at auction to an anonymous buyer and is said to be available for rent. Today, the use of a labia stretcher in courtrooms is so unusual that it must be flown in the night before by the Air Force. With the more common, almost taken for granted scrotum stretchings in todays courts, it isn't unusual for the judge to order the husband to pull in the A frame himself, struggling and groaning, while wearing a leather harness designed specifically for the task. The humiliated husband must then wait while the bailiff anchors the supporting dolly to ringbolts in the floor. Predatory females love this performance and gloat with anticipation. Recently the practice has been slightly abated, however, with the introduction of the newer, lightweight aluminum A frames. The stretching is the husband's introduction to his new status in life: A Human Pop-Up Target. Whenever she pushes the buzzer, he automatically clangs into position. She may then fire at will.

Welcome Home

Q. I spent five years as a P.O.W. in Vietnam, hanging upside down on a meat hook. Despite the beatings and torture, I made it home, married, and purchased a new home. Now, in her divorce suit against me, my wife is claiming half the money I earned in Vietnam—as a P.O.W.!

A. It appears you "commingled" your Vietnam pay when you bought the new house. This "commingling" is a popular term for the legal profession's method of increasing awards to divorcing wives. Incidentally, there's a new law, passed by Congress, giving the previously sacrosanct military retirements to ex-wives. They've even established a national hotline in Washington that a veteran's ex-spouse can call, free of charge, and determine what percentage of his retirement she's now entitled to.

Q. Will it ever end?

A. Marriage, being the only offense for which you may be tried continuously, dictates that its ferocious punitive aspects should never be underestimated. Years after your divorce, you may be repeatedly hauled into court under the spectre of fines, jail, and seizure of wages and property. These suits may also be instituted under the names of your children (possibly at the prodding of your ex-wife) as separate litigants!

No Satisfaction

Q. The judge cleaned me out, gave my wife everything in the divorce, and now she grumbles about having been short changed. How do you explain that?

A. The predatory female is never satisfied with her blessings. She always wants more. When the judge began bestowing money and property on her, he became, in a sense, her new benefactor replacing you. Now the resentment and ingratitude formerly reserved for her husband may also be directed at the judge. The predatory female traditionally bites the hand that feeds her. She is capable of lashing out at you, the judge, your attorney, her attorney, your family, her new husband or boyfriend, and legions of others for years to come.

New Quarters

Q. It really frosts me to see my ex-wife living regally, sometimes with other men, in the home I was evicted from, while I have to exist in a sleazy apartment with rented furniture, overlooking the freeway, next door to three families of illegal aliens, and directly above a noisy Dempsey dumpster.

A. Wait until your kids inform you that her new boyfriend is overhauling his Harley Davidson "fat bob" in the living room. Each year the news media shows a few weeping and wailing women standing in front of their flooded or burned homes, after some natural catastrophe. The governor flies over and declares the neighborhood a disaster area, making low cost loans available to them. The Red Cross and civic groups respond. But also, each year, thousands of divorcing men not only lose their homes, but their children—and much future income including their retirements—through the matriarchal legal process. And guess what? Nobody says a thing. The news media isn't there with microphones, and no one gives a tinker's damn.

Public Property

Q. Aren't these one sided divorces killing the family system, or at least discouraging perceptive men from marrying?
A. Yes, and that's why you see the matriarchal system going to absurdities like palimony suits. Most states claim a public policy of preserving marriages and families on one hand, while on the other, through the matriarchal system, make it financially attractive for predatory females to dump their husbands. This is like handing a flame thrower to a pyromaniac. The result is that we are up to our armpits in divorces, and the divorce industry has grown to a multi-billion dollar enterprise. We're a nation of litigants with the

courts saying, in effect, "Ok Mr., go ahead and marry, but if she exercises the most famous of all women's prerogatives—changing her mind—we'll help her clean your clock. We'll give her your home, children, retirement, and much of your pay check for years to come. You'll even have to pay her attorney." Remember, this message isn't for the indigent or very rich, only the majority of males. Although seldom done, the smart man familiarizes himself with the ground rules before binding himself to the terms of legal matrimony.

> "I'm like the Statue of Liberty. Nobody wants to pay the cost to maintain me, but everybody wants to say he's been there."
>
> —*Priscilla Davis*

The Exceptions

Q. Are there any exceptions to these divorce disasters?

A. Certainly. There are wives who choose not to exercise their power and simply want out. There are many women who don't need the crutch of the matriarchal system to provide for themselves. For whatever reason, some men escape divorce devastation when the wife lets them go, lets them off the hook. The little field mouse, having been trapped, is set free in the woods.

126

The Women's Side

Q. Do you have a constructive suggestion for the young woman who hasn't yet married?
A. Consider how degrading it is to depend solely on someone else for support. There is an alternative to "Mr. Wonderful" that can give you great personal satisfaction, a feeling of accomplishment. Get a career. Make something of yourself financially. Don't become dependent for the rest of your life on somebody that you may not even like in a few years.

Matriarchal Judiciary

Q. How can judges be so blatantly pro-female?
A. Your description is accurate. To this date, the public record demands that most judges be classified as pro-female. They are elected officials and women control the vote. Have you ever heard of the League of *Men* Voters or the National Organization for *Men?* The matriarchal society will not long tolerate a judge who doesn't lean toward women. If he strays far from the party line they'll have him removed, or at least attempt it. The predatory females of our society, the controlling factor, want jurists who understand that children need their mothers at the "tender age," because they'll soon be too old for indoctrination into the matriarchal thinking process. In fact, the matriarchy has deposed judges for a

single careless remark, deemed anti-feminist.

Children

Q. The courts have taken my children away from me. I see them when allowed, but my little boy hides under the bed or in a closet when it's time to go back to his mother. The resulting scene is heartbreaking. Do you have any general suggestions?

A. Children are expendable to a predatory female. They come second. You may be, even without custody, your kids' only real hope. It's not uncommon for an ex-wife to subject your children to serious surgery, for example, without ever informing you. Insist on seeing them regularly, never fail to pick them up on time, never promise anything you can't deliver, and never say anything bad to them about their mother. Some men, knowing the materialistic truths about predatory females, have successfully purchased their children. You might consider offering her an additional sum of money per month (contractual alimony) or a lump sum. Predatory females are very concerned about social stigma, so to facilitate the transaction and provide her with an avenue for approval by her friends, you may have to disguise the purchase in some manner.

"Happiness is finding a picture of your ex-wife on a shopping bag"

—Airline Pilot

It Never Ends

Q. Do predatory females sue men in their graves?

A. Death is no protection from a predatory female. They commonly sue a man's estate and have even been known to knock the gold fillings from their husbands' teeth before the mortician arrives.

Plateaus

Q. Are there discernible levels of recovery from a divorce?

A. There are four noteworthy plateaus.

   1. *Indignation and Disbelief:* This is the shock stage. The male can't believe how powerless and pathetic he is in the face of the matriarchal court system. His ego is severely damaged. His wife sits there and smirks while he loses everything including his home and family. He sees evil amusement in her eyes as the judge orders in the "scrotum stretcher" and makes him pay *her* attorney's fees. He realizes that his entire married life was a con job. For the first time he feels the impact of the nationwide matrimonial sting operation. He winces at the thought of how eagerly he took the bait. Nobody likes to admit they've been hustled.

2. *Bitter Acceptance:* He has no choice but to accept humiliating defeat from a predatory female and her protective matriarchal system. He resigns himself to his fate, but he is angry. Often he begins searching frantically for another woman in a pitiful attempt to rebuild his self-esteem.

3. *Grudging Cynicism:* He is back on the playing field again, recovering from injuries, but is still resentful and has become cynical about love and marriage. He begins to suspect the existence of a dark, predatory side of the female.

4. *Humorous Cynicism:* The active bitterness has died and he jokes about traits of the predatory female and the matriarchal system. He knows the modus operandi of predatory females. He enjoys watching them work and appreciates their efforts for what they are.

Some men, trying desperately to reestablish themselves through another woman, never reach the last two plateaus. These unfortunates are usually condemned to repeat their odyssey of marital self-sacrifice.

"Those who cannot remember the past are condemned to repeat it."

—*George Santayana*

Custodial Case

Q. Should newly divorced men avoid making big decisions for awhile?

A. It takes at least one year to convalesce from the A frame. Performance at full mental capacity is not normally possible after a scrotum stretching. One tends to make mistakes that later seem preposterous. After a divorce, huge financial blunders aren't common because normally there isn't any money left to squander. Emotional blunders are, however, quite prevalent. Charging into the ring with another female, desperately trying to fill a vacuum, is always a tragic mistake.

Haggling

Q. How does the new girlfriend get along with the ex-wife?

A. This can be one of the more interesting scenarios for observing predatory females. Competition for a man's paychecks, property, and other goods and chattels can be violent. Imagine a cartoon with two witches going at it tooth and nail, changing each other into hop toads, slinging fireballs, transforming themselves into dragons, snakes, and wolverines. This battle of the dinosaurs may last for years while the man meekly submits his paycheck to a gnashing and tearing between predatory females.

"Men are nothing but grab bags for women."

— *F. Scott Fitzgerald*

Lifeline

Q. I wish I had this book before I got married. My ex-wife, a Sloan Ranger, is so mean that I avoid her at all costs.

A. Yes, this field guide could have kept your balls off the damp grass. But at least you seem to have learned a basic rule about ex-wives: No kindness from you will ever go unpunished.

Let It Rest

Q. Rev. Shannon, do you have any comments for divorced women?

A. Only to quote the immortal words of Hoveden:

"Stir not the embers with the sword."

FREEDOM

"Women are like tricks by sleight of hand,
which to admire, we should not understand."

– William Congreve – 1692

The Lesson

Q. I was wiped out in my divorce. Is there anything good about that?

A. A dog that chases cars and only gets nicked will be back for more. A dog that is slammed to the pavement and injured may learn his lesson. The fellow who skates through his divorce, escaping relatively unscathed, often doesn't learn. He returns for a rematch, sometimes several, until he is physically and financially devastated. Don't dot the landscape, as many do, with failed marriages and broken families. Savor your opportunity to learn the first time; don't repeat mistakes.

Repeat Performance

Q. Who remarries? Idiots?

A. Two basic types of men come back for

seconds. One is Mr. Nice Guy. He just can't believe that other people aren't as loving and ingenuous as he is. When he hears about a particularly nasty divorce, he automatically assumes there are facts justifying the vindictiveness of the female. He can't imagine it happening to him. The second type is the man who HAS TO BE MARRIED. He is a custodial case, unable to function without a woman occupying a position of power in his life. This is due to his religion, upbringing, or other deep rooted motivation for him to marry. You will sometimes encounter this individual on the threshold of another wedding. He presents a pathetic, even false cheerfulness. He is beyond the point of no return—again—and his eyes are glassed over. Advice would neither be welcomed nor heeded. He will soon have another monster in his home and is doomed to a lifetime of subjection and acquiescence.

Odds

Q. What are my chances of recovery from a divorce?
A. Your chances improve by coming out of a short marriage, being young, having good earning potential, no children, no other divorces, and a good working perception of predatory females. Your chances decrease with your being old, retired, married a long

time, having limited earning potential, being a victim of other marriages and lacking a proper perception of predatory females. The longer your unprotected, uneducated exposure to predatory females continues, the greater disaster may befall you.

Resolutions

Q. How do I keep from repeating the same suicidal blunders with another woman?
A. Know your adversary. Know that she IS your adversary. Develop a working understanding of predatory females. Accept what you've learned about predatory females, both emotionally and intellectually. Forget your past presumptions and values concerning females. They were sprinkled into your mind by the matriarchal system. You have to break out.

The Beginning

Q. How do I re-program myself?
A. Condition yourself physically and mentally. Most people look like gunnysacks full of doorknobs. This is partially due to heavy doses of dependency on predatory females. Work out every day and get yourself into good physical shape. Take up a sport and start running. Do what predatory females have done for thousands of years—concentrate completely on yourself. Rid your mind

of the garbage dumped into it by the matriarchal society. Occupy it instead with good books, films, and a hobby that benefits you, that you enjoy. If you get horny, don't play the matriarchal society's hackneyed dating game, RENT a woman. For two or three hundred dollars you can rent a sexual partner skilled enough to turn you into a boiled chicken. Spare yourself the tedious sales pitch that accompanies dating. There is no such thing as a free lunch, *period.*

Sex

Q. What about sex?
A. For the male, the worst is usually fantastic, as the humor goes, but is it really that great? Most often not. For starters, many women are orgasmically dysfunctional, incapable of orgasm, making them little more than spectators. Why do you think Woody Allen wrote lines about his jaw getting sore? Unfortunately, finding a truly first class sex partner is a tall order. You're dealing with an extremely small percentage of the available females. Anything else and you're going steerage, strictly third rate. For the risks involved, you'd definitely be better off with a high class prostitute. After all, there are good reasons, most of them very Darwinian, for prostitution being the oldest profession. We're talking survival here. Banned and hunted by the matriarchal society because they threaten the

136

established marital scam, prostitutes are not only legal in some jurisdictions, but may be the wisest investment for your dating dollar.

Games

Q. I'm tired of games and sometimes totally indifferent to females, even on dates. This seems to make them more aggressive. Increasingly, I find myself curious only as to how she will arrive at a foregone conclusion.
A. You already know that a predatory female, when confronted with indifference, usually finds it intolerable. Unfortunately, game playing between the sexes is now so vicious that, by the time people achieve proficiency, they are often burned out and no longer desirable.

Current Events

Q. Is it just me, or are women getting meaner and more bad tempered?
A. A lot of people, including women, are beginning to say that. We live in a society of tough, career oriented females who smoke cigars, wear neckties, and seem determined to prove something. After some critical age they grow noticeably meaner or downright unpleasant. They will go out of their way to be rude, and they will nurture confrontations. The phenomenon is particularly noticeable

with females working in service industries that deal with the public.

Q. Why is it that people will invariably say, "Well, you married her," or "you're just bitter" when they learn the facts of your divorce?

A. It's a way of transferring the focus to you, a subconscious, protective reflex that allows them to avoid thinking it could happen to them or, worse, that they might be part of the unholy process. After all, things are getting worse, not better, out there. Guys are disappearing, mysteriously, from the country with their retirement monies which they have "stolen." One fellow recently ran a bulldozer through his house that was supposedly being awarded to the wife. Kids ask daddy why their pictures are on the milk carton and, shortly thereafter, daddy's on his way to prison. He had "stolen" his own children.

A New Perspective

Q. Following your advice, my relationship with females would be on an entirely new basis.

A. True. As you slowly re-program yourself, you notice the advantage of a new perspective. The previously somewhat concealed servitude of your fellow males, especially the married ones, begins to glare obnoxiously. You find it at once disgusting and alarming.

You suddenly realize that you've broken the code of the predatory female; you've crossed the line and can never go back. You are demanding more performance. You see how most acquisitive females run on a short loop. The same old con game, played over and over, becomes disappointing and boring. It lets you down. You are angered to think that you subjected yourself to such tedium only to risk discovering a huge seed wart on the end of your crank a week later. Your ability to discern predatory females, especially the "crazies," becomes increasingly acute, even with the briefest encounters. The effects of being slammed violently each month, from one end of the PH scale to the other, begins to show on the predatory females you encounter. Their nervous preoccupation and darting eyes become all too familiar to you. When seeing the haughty conceit of a non-acquisitive female, you rejoice at not being her victim. You are thankful for the transparency of predatory females to the trained eye. However, accompanied by your new perspective is the knowledge that some of the thrill of "going into the lion's cage" is gone forever. This is always a by-product of being perceptive of the predatory female, of having taken her measure. The inept or unskilled predatory females are especially disheartening. They stumble through their act, embarrassing everyone. Unconvincingly, they suppress their own needs in attempts to please you, resulting only in your feeling sorry for them. Or, at the other extreme, they may try to control you through denial. Denial, used by religion for years, works best with untrained, ignorant people. The predatory female tries to make the victim feel guilty and plays on his good manners or stupidity not to rebuke her. Denial is usually combined with some type of sexual teasing. Angling for control, some weak minded predatory females use the ploy of objecting to profanity or ribaldry under the guise of being "respected." These self-appointed moralists like to make others feel inferior and may hold the entire evening's good will as hostage to their scoldings. Like other game players, such individuals are in oversupply and are time wasters. You will begin to find, with your new perspective, that someone you can take seriously, a truly captivating and beautiful woman—a long ball hitter, is extremely rare. Indeed, they are rare enough to demand almost any price and get it.

The Church

Q. Is there a refuge (from predatory females) in the church? Might one find, in a church, an innocent flower dedicated to being a submissive, biblical wife, or have the churches failed to meet the challenges to marriage and family presented by predatory females?

A. Having dropped the ball completely, the churches, particularly on this issue, are in total disgrace. While dangling the scent of forbidden sex (the denial technique) under the noses of impressionable youth, churches all over the country are pushing marriage as a sanctified nirvana. They do nothing to educate their young members about one of the most dangerous parts of marriage: the enforceable aspects of the contract. Greedily insensitive to the times, and ignoring the ferocious legal implications, churches continue selling marriage while treating young nuptials as though they'd won first prize on a game show. Unfortunately, despite all the fancy wrapping, underneath lies the same old nasty contract with the state, the liabilities and humiliations for the husband. Churches are crawling with predatory females masquerading as born again lilies of the field, but ravenously seeking willing, naive males. Those who bite on the biblical "lord and master" routine being peddled by churchgoing predatory females, being more deluded than most, will find (after the camel gets its head in the tent) their scrotum stretchings twice as miserable.

The Long Ball Hitter

Q. I am 35 years old, divorced, a millionaire, athletic, a member of numerous social and benefit organizations, a fugitive from several marriage minded girls, but completely bored where women are concerned. I settled for second best when I married my former wife and I'll never make that mistake again. I'm tired of all these second stringers and would like an affair with one real long ball hitter before I'm too old.

A. The type of woman you refer to, a long ball hitter, is a rare commodity. As you become increasingly tired of stupidity, cheap shot maneuvering, cat boxes, lies, poor performances, and incipient "penis wisdom," curtailment of relations with women is often preferable to another ordinary relationship. Further, these common, everyday females, many lacking even basic good manners, are often just as expensive as a rare, star performer. Your extensive experience with predatory females has hardened you, made you less impressionable. You know too much. The hiring of a prostitute may seem a welcome relief to the mediocrity of dating. Only a high class, beautiful, agile, independent, and intuitive woman will ever be able to ring your bell again. Don't expect to go deaf from all the noise . . . they are few and far between.

Players

Q. Having been single a long time, I nearly married one of our corporate attorneys last year when I was thirty six. I was rescued solely by the accidental discovery that she was occasionally sleeping with her uncle in New York.

But for that windfall, I would have been trapped and put on exhibit in the public square with other married men. I am now happily resigned to remaining off the playing field, watching the fracas from the bleachers and, if a truly remarkable female makes her debut, running down for a quick scrimmage. I would suggest this alternative to anyone who is tired of the daily slamming of heads—the frantic grinding that occurs in the field.

A. You have arrived at the eventual hiding place of most men who have experienced the predatory female, learned something, but still enjoy the game. Most, like yourself, prefer the exhilarating breath of freedom to the sack cloth and ashes that accompany a "commitment." In the end, a predatory female, no matter how beautiful, will always be the succubus: exciting, momentarily thrilling, mesmerizing—but dangerous as a green mamba.

> "For every beautiful woman, somewhere there is a man who is tired of her."
>
> —*Lawrence Bostwick Shannon*

The Veteran vs. The Novitiate

Q. The other night I was mounting a woman, preparatory to intercourse, when suddenly I burst out in hysterics and couldn't stop laughing. I was struck by the absurdity of the scene. The woman became extremely angry and stormed out, slamming the door. I have since been unable to take a woman seriously.

A. A vacation from predatory females is recommended. You have battle fatigue. This often happens. You wish you didn't know now what you didn't know then. For you, the phenomenon of waking in the night to a face that is strangely and supernaturally different from the one you went to bed with is not new. You are no longer shocked when a girlfriend announces that she'll be married in a month, even though she doesn't know anyone, and a month later—wham! She's married. You are jaded to the fact that your own attorney doesn't really care about your case and is sympathetic to the opposition. The ring bolts in the courtroom floor, used for anchoring the scrotum stretcher dolly, are old hat to you. A single reading of *The Predatory Female* will suffice in your case, but for the neophyte, the lamb of innocence who supports the matriarchy, the cupcake who doesn't believe the message in these pages, another reading is prescribed.

"With all my worldly goods I thee endow."

— *Solemnization of Matrimony*
Book of Common Prayer

Deliverance

Q. Reverend Shannon, how successful do

you think this book will be in saving its
readers from the talons of predatory females?
A. I see it as strictly a function of how much
they are willing to believe. People only believe
what they want to. Facts and reason have
never been of great importance to those caught
in the supernatural spell of a predatory female.
As we have seen, her victims become incapable
of reason. They don't want to be rescued.
They resist efforts to save them in much the
same manner that a victim of a cult religious
brainwashing resists being deprogrammed.
There is little question that the psychological
grip of a predatory female upon her prey is
worthy of Satan himself, despite evidence that
a treacherous heart and a lying tongue may be
the natural weapons of a subjagated sex.
Either way, we will never know the immeasur-
able damage done by predatory females to the
families, the children, the sanity, and the
futures of those who have plunged, often with
innocent enthusiasm, into her web. Though
the truth about predatory females isn't what
everyone wants to hear, the wise will listen. To
the rest go our sympathies because, for them,
in courtrooms around the nation, the scrotum
stretchers are waiting.

"The wrath of a woman is much to dread."
         — *Tristram and Ysolt*

"The most persistent hate is that which doth degenerate from love."
         — *Map, De Nugis Curialium*

"A married man is a guy walking a tightrope, balancing dangerously while his smirking wife and her amused friends pull and shake the rope."

"Keeping is compromising."
         — *Capt. James Lockridge*

SECTION II

SURVIVAL GUIDES

Danger Signals

The following are selected danger signals to be aware of when consorting with predatory females. These signals will help you identify her as predatory and warn you of impending moves in her favor.

- She asks questions such as: "What about us? What about our future? Where are we going?"
- She leaves personal effects in your home.
- She thinks it's ok to shoplift.
- She calls your kitchen "my kitchen."
- Her mother is an attorney.
- She's on a first name basis with her pharmacist.
- She has a cat.
- She has the TV schedule memorized.
- She wants to meet your family.
- She lies in bed until noon.
- She buys you clothes.
- She suggests that you leave bigger tips.
- She steals from her employer.
- She tells you how much better everything would be if you were married to her.
- She belongs to a women's rights group.
- She chews tobacco.
- She has a tattoo.
- She parties with her friends after work while her kids are still in day-care.
- She has a mantra.

- She inquires about your will.
- She gives you an ultimatum.
- She is offended if you suggest going dutch.
- She rearranges your kitchen or bedroom closet.
- She arrives unannounced at your home with groceries.
- She wants you to take her to church.
- She introduces herself as your wife, mistress, or fiancée.
- She always wants to borrow your car.
- She wants a key to your home.
- She makes toll calls on your phone without asking.
- She is partial to TV dramas centered around doctors or hospitals.
- She has previously attempted suicide.
- She berates you for not buying something because "you make so much money," or "you can afford it."
- She receives payments from an ex-husband or boyfriend.
- She sneaks looks through your wallet or other personal items.
- She affects a foreign accent.
- She corresponds heavily with girlfriends.
- She spends a lot of time with her mother.
- She wants to know your sign.
- She pulls her suitcase on a little cart.
- She sees an analyst.
- Her mother is suing her father.
- She's on a first-name basis with the piano player at Nordstrom.

- She objects to your profanity.
- She makes frequent doctors' appointments.
- You find yourself trying to ignore things that you don't like about her.
- She wears a rape whistle or carries mace.
- She practices karate kicks to the gonads of a man's silhouette pinned to her bedroom wall.
- She makes midweek luncheon dates with you and arrives with two or three of her secretarial friends and/or her mother.
- She gives her car a pet name.
- She hangs a "today is the first day of the rest of your life" poster in your bathroom.
- She has "Love is . . ." cartoons on her refrigerator door.
- She has your holidays and weekends planned without having consulted you.
- She goes into shock when you announce plans for a weekend ski trip with your buddies.
- She "cleans" your house, throwing out magazines and other items objectionable to her.
- You find yourself doing things, at her behest, that you don't want to do.
- Her cooking ability is limited to casseroles, lasagna, and quiche.
- Her refrigerator is full of science projects and yours resembles a two week old church potluck dinner.
- She has more than her share of yeast infections.

- She wears sunglasses with small rhinestone hearts on the lenses.
- She mentions having "invested" a certain amount of time in a previous or current boyfriend.
- Your bathroom wastebasket is constantly full of wadded up tissue paper, string, kleenex, and cardboard tubes.
- You get a lecture on gun control when she discovers a pistol in your nightstand.
- You find her douche bag hanging in your shower.
- She uses the words "but I'm worth it."

Extreme Danger Signals

Any of the following signals could indicate a predatory female that should be considered an immediate threat.

- She is careless about birth control.
- She has a brass rivet in her nose.
- The picture on her driver's license is not her.
- She wants to look at baby clothes when you're shopping together.
- She calls you by your full given name.
- Her mother is a judge.
- Her medicine cabinet looks like a pharmacy.
- She has several cats.

- She takes sides with waiters and clerks if you protest the bill or service.
- She receives payments from an ex, but is suing for more.
- When with her, you have the feeling of being followed.
- She practices writing her signature using your last name.
- You awaken in the middle of the night to find her staring at you.

You Are About to Be Dumped

The following are signs that indicate a strong possibility of your imminent sacking. You have run out the clock.

- She frequently rearranges the furniture in your home, moving even the heaviest objects.
- You return home after a brief trip to find her acting strange and distant.
- She is often lost in thought and wants to take classes or get a job.
- She insists on going to the post office herself to collect the mail.
- She no longer bothers to clean up the kitchen or other areas of the house.
- She openly flirts with other men.

- She brazenly suggests that you buy her some expensive item.
- She loudly breaks wind while dining with your parents or when sleeping with you.
- She opts for late TV instead of going to bed with you.
- She is constantly with her relatives or friends, ignoring you.
- She is increasingly unavailable to do what you want to do.
- She asks, in a way suggesting approval, if you are sleeping with anyone else.

Suggestions For Engineering Your Own Dumping

- Leave stingy tips in restaurants.
- Put locks on your telephones.
- During a party she gives for you to meet her friends, fall asleep and snore loudly.
- Clad only in a jockstrap, greet her parents at the door to her apartment.
- Laugh hysterically every time you see a dead cat.
- Start asking her to go "dutch."
- Tell her you have a metal plate in your head.
- Purchase a life size, inflatable sex doll and keep it in your bedroom.

- Introduce her using an incorrect name. When she protests, act confused and apologize, but do it again a week later.
- Start forgetting holidays and birthdays.
- When dining out formally, throw your head back and noisily gargle your drink.
- Arrive at her class reunion dressed in an Easter Bunny suit with a large, oversized, strap-on dildo. Leaping wildly, run through the crowd and stick your dildo in the punch bowl.
- Smelling of cheap whiskey, show up drunk at all family events.
- Start being possessive. Call her constantly; demand to know where she's been. Hover over her so when she dumps you, it's final.

Glossary of Terms and Phrases (commonly used by the predatory female)

YOU ARE THE ONLY ONE I CARE ABOUT.
You are the best candidate she's found thus far to become her lifetime, unpaid male butler. If you keep up the good work, she'll enroll you in doggie obedience school.

YOU ARE THE ONLY MAN I'VE EVER REALLY LOVED.

A blatant lie. This kind of statement comes during a final, desperate attempt to lock you into a lifetime of servitude and is never heard after the wedding.

I WANT YOU TO MEET MY FAMILY.

She doesn't want you to meet her family, she wants them to meet you to evaluate your financial prospects.

WHAT'S YOUR SIGN?

A question asked by predatory females of the lower mental classifications. Other character- istics of this type of woman are: (1) They end every sentence with the words "you know." (2) They name their cars. (3) They chew bub- ble gum (4) They periodically say with in- dignation "Don't classify me!"

YOU ARE GOING TO END UP A LONELY OLD MAN.

You have refused to allow her to con you into the matrimonial hustle and she resents you for it.

I'D RATHER GET TO KNOW YOU FIRST.

This can mean any or all of the following: (1) She wants to further evaluate your financial and social status before dumping her current lover who she's been cheating on for the last six months. (2) In her haste to avoid last week's boyfriend, she left the apartment without showering and smells like a tuna boat. (3) Her husband won't leave on his business trip for a couple of days (she may suggest calling later). (4) She is meeting your roommate at a motel in forty five minutes.

WHAT DO YOU DO?
Probably the most common question posed by the predatory female in a social setting. A quickie audit of your financial potential.

CAN'T WE DO SOMETHING ALONE FOR A CHANGE?
You aren't accessible enough when protected by friends and loved ones.

THERE'S NO ROOM IN YOUR LIFE FOR A WOMAN.
You have already been replaced; she has given up on controlling you.

ARE YOU MARRIED?
Are you the only one spending your money?

ARE YOU DIVORCED?
If you fell once, you could fall again. Predators are always attracted to the vulnerable.

ALL YOU CARE ABOUT IS MY BODY.
Usually spoken in a resentful tone for two

reasons: (1) She's right. (2) So far she has realized less than anticipated reward for her services.

FORGET WHAT'S HAPPENED IN THE PAST, IT'S NOW THAT'S IMPORTANT.
Quit thinking about the alimony check you just wrote and the cute kids you used to think were yours. Let your guard down.

I AGREE, WE SHOULD LIVE TOGETHER FIRST.
It's easier to get the camel's head into the tent first. Let the rest of her follow later.

I DON'T BELIEVE IN LIVING WITH A MAN OUT OF WEDLOCK.
Joint checking and saving accounts are a prerequisite for the nuptial bliss that comes with having sex once every six weeks.

WILL I SEE YOU AGAIN?
Am I going to get another shot at your wallet?

I'M NOT THAT KIND OF GIRL.
Pure donkey dung. An hour ago she was at the gynecologist's office letting a perfect stranger finger fuck her in the name of modern medicine.

I'M NOT IN THE HABIT OF DOING THIS.
Nonsense. Her last boyfriend told you she

could suck a tennis ball through fifty feet of garden hose.

I DON'T GO AWAY FOR THE WEEKEND WITH STRANGE MEN.

Another example of the virginity complex. In reality she's been porked by every trucker from Abilene to Barstow.

I'M LOOKING FOR A STABLE, MATURE, KIND, RESPONSIBLE MAN WHO IS FINANCIALLY SECURE, CONSIDERATE OF MY NEEDS, GIVES ME MY OWN SPACE, AND SHARES MY INTERESTS.

Another self-centered predatory female, totally lacking in originality, who gets her lines from the "personal" ads in the local singles rag. This is a girl who demands her support payments on time and will expect you to be cheerful about it.

COME ON IN, I'LL JUST BE A MINUTE.

I am purposely late so you can get accustomed to waiting for me like a chauffeur.

YOU DON'T KNOW HOW LUCKY YOU ARE. YOU HAVE REALLY GOT IT MADE.

How have you managed to elude marital bliss for so long? (sometimes used as a throwaway line to make you feel superior, over-

confident, and possibly increase your
vulnerability)

**DON'T WORRY ABOUT ME, I'M JUST
GLAD IT WAS GOOD FOR YOU.**
Thank God it's over. Now maybe I can talk
him into dinner at Chasen's.

**SORRY, I WAITED ALL DAY FOR YOU
TO CALL AND NOW I HAVE OTHER
PLANS.**
Ridiculous. She is simply sour grapes at
having failed to transform you into a nema-
tode who begs for sexual crumbs.

**YOU DON'T INTERFERE WITH MY
SPACE. I'M REALLY GLAD YOU KNOW
WHO YOU ARE AND WHAT YOU
WANT. YOU'RE IN A REAL GOOD
PLACE RIGHT NOW.**
She's a graduate of one of the several self-
awareness scams going around the country.
This type of mental midget is capable of draw-
ing in a three hundred dollar per month billing
from a door-to-door soap company.

I WISH I HAD MET YOU YEARS AGO.
An old standard automatically issued to each
new boyfriend. As a matter of fact, you did
meet when you were working your way
through college as a shoe clerk, but she
wouldn't give you the time of day.

I WANT TO REALIZE MY FULL
POTENTIAL BEFORE I SETTLE DOWN.
I want to try bagging a real fat bank account
before I settle for yours.

I WANT TO FIND MY IDENTITY, TO BE
ME, TO DISCOVER MYSELF.
I'm tired of being a housewife and a mother
and I want to make it with some college guys.

I DON'T WANT OUR RELATIONSHIP TO
BECOME STAGNANT.
The blow job to dining out ratio is below
standards, the campaign to move in with you
is losing momentum, or she just met a sixty
five year old multi-millionaire who's good for
at least a car and a condo.

YOU HATE WOMEN, DON'T YOU.
You just finished telling her the reason God
created women was because sheep don't do
windows.

OUR RELATIONSHIP ISN'T GOING
ANYWHERE.
Choose from the following: (1) She just made
the mistake of introducing you to her mother.
(2) Her younger sister received a diamond
engagement ring for Christmas and you gave
her a tennis racket. (3) She's angry because
you forgot to lock the bedroom door and
your roommate came in to borrow a tie during

coitus. (4) You got drunk at her brother's bar mitzvah and announced that she looked exceptionally well for a girl who just had an abortion.

DON'T CATEGORIZE ME, I'M NOT LIKE OTHER WOMEN.
You are hearing the faint scraping of the asp moving inside the wicker basket. You have tinkered with the latch and should consider yourself lucky to have so far escaped serious harm. Flee while you can.

I'M NOT A LOOSE WOMAN.
If that's true, why is there an "On Deck Circle" painted on her bedroom floor?

WE NEED TO HAVE A TALK.
You haven't been as obedient as her roommate's boyfriend and it's becoming socially embarrassing for her.

YOU'RE NOT THE PERSON YOU WERE WHEN WE MET.
The Walt Disney ending to your affair that she and her pedestrian friends expected did not materialize. Moreover, you've stopped grinning stupidly while she makes long distance calls from your phone.

YOU'RE VERY GOOD FOR ME.
You are the only one I've met recently who'll

indulge my whims with his wallet and wait on me hand and foot.

YOU CAN HAVE ANYBODY YOU WANT, WHY DID YOU PICK ME?

Standard throwaway line to spot check your capacity for reason after being given a bite of the apple.

YOU HAVE A LOT OF EXPLAINING TO DO.

She enjoys a lover's quarrel and likes to feel wronged. This very statement indicates you are in big trouble already. She's angling for a good groveling to tell her friends about.

HOW DO YOU DEFINE OUR RELATIONSHIP?

She is looking for a progress report on her skills at conning you into a real stupid decision.

WHEN CAN I MEET YOUR PARENTS?

I'm going to need your mother's support in safety wiring your scrotum to the marital pegboard.

HOW OLD ARE YOU?

Will I be able to cash in on your best years?

YOU'RE SO CHEAP.

Why should I tolerate your reluctance to

spend money when virtual armies of men can't wait to dump their wallets in my lap. What would my friends say?

YOU AREN'T CARING AND SENSITIVE.
You don't show the proper enthusiasm when reminded to open doors for her, take out the trash, empty her cat box, or carry her packages. Further, you don't grin like a gibbon ape while she orders a seventy-five dollar bottle of wine at dinner.

I SENSE A DISTANCE BETWEEN YOU AND MOTHER.
You have just met "Mother" and receive a rude reminder that, with age, everything does get bigger, hairier and closer to the ground.

YOU'RE PUTTING LIMITS ON OUR RELATIONSHIP.
YOU ARE UNABLE TO COMPROMISE.
YOU REFUSE TO NORMALIZE OUR RELATIONSHIP.
You won't consent to her living independently on your bank account, with no accountability whatsoever.

Bibliography and Suggested Reading

Made In Heaven, Settled In Court
−Marvin Mitchelson

The Taming Of The Shrew
−William Shakespeare

Little Big Man *−Thomas Berger*

How I found Freedom In An Unfree World
−Harry Browne

The Manipulated Man *−Ester Villar*

Male-Practice *−Dr. Robert Mendelshon*

Fools Die *−Mario Puzo*

For your convenience in ordering additional copies of *The Predatory Female* or *The Mother*, just fill out the form below and mail to:

Banner Books
P.O. Box 70302
Reno, NV 89570

Please send me_____copies of *The Predatory Female* by Rev. Lawrence Shannon at $8.95 each and_____copies of *The Mother - A Suburban Horror Story* at $8.95 each (quantity discounts available) to:

Name _____

Address _____

City _____

State _____ Zip _____

Subtotal_____

Shipping & Handling $4.95 per order_____
(orders over $20.00 add 10%)

Total _____

(Send check or money order, no cash or C.O.D.)

Visit us at: http://www.vegastar.com/Banner/